GnuPG - Using the GNU Privacy Guard

A catalogue record for this book is available from the Hong Kong Public Libraries.

Published in Hong Kong by Samurai Media Limited.

Email: info@samuraimedia.org

ISBN 978-988-8381-15-9

This is the The GNU Privacy Guard Manual (version 2.1.9, October 2015).
Published by The GnuPG Project
https://gnupg.org
(or http://ic6au7wa3f6naxjq.onion)

Background Cover Image by https://www.flickr.com/people/webtreatsetc/

Short Contents

Table of Contents

1 A short installation guide.

Unfortunately the installation guide has not been finished in time. Instead of delaying the release of GnuPG 2.0 even further, I decided to release without that guide. The chapter on gpg-agent and gpgsm do include brief information on how to set up the whole thing. Please watch the GnuPG website for updates of the documentation. In the meantime you may search the GnuPG mailing list archives or ask on the gnupg-users mailing listsfor advise on how to solve problems or how to get that whole thing up and running.

** Building the software

Building the software is decribed in the file 'INSTALL'. Given that you are already reading this documentation we can only give some extra hints

To comply with the rules on GNU systems you should have build time configured gnupg using:

```
./configure --sysconfdir=/etc --localstatedir=/var
```

This is to make sure that system wide configuration files are searched in the directory '/etc' and variable data below '/var'; the default would be to also install them below '/usr/local' where the binaries get installed. If you selected to use the '--prefix=/' you obviously don't need those option as they are the default then.

** Notes on setting a root CA key to trusted

X.509 is based on a hierarchical key infrastructure. At the root of the tree a trusted anchor (root certificate) is required. There are usually no other means of verifying whether this root certificate is trustworthy than looking it up in a list. GnuPG uses a file ('trustlist.txt') to keep track of all root certificates it knows about. There are 3 ways to get certificates into this list:

- Use the list which comes with GnuPG. However this list only contains a few root certificates. Most installations will need more.

- Let gpgsm ask you whether you want to insert a new root certificate. This feature is enabled by default; you may disable it using the option 'no-allow-mark-trusted' into 'gpg-agent.conf'.

- Manually maintain the list of trusted root certificates. For a multi user installation this can be done once for all users on a machine. Specific changes on a per-user base are also possible.

2 Invoking GPG-AGENT

`gpg-agent` is a daemon to manage secret (private) keys independently from any protocol. It is used as a backend for `gpg` and `gpgsm` as well as for a couple of other utilities.

The agent is automatically started on demand by `gpg`, `gpgsm`, `gpgconf`, or `gpg-connect-agent`. Thus there is no reason to start it manually. In case you want to use the included Secure Shell Agent you may start the agent using:

    gpg-connect-agent /bye

You should always add the following lines to your `.bashrc` or whatever initialization file is used for all shell invocations:

    GPG_TTY=$(tty)
    export GPG_TTY

It is important that this environment variable always reflects the output of the `tty` command. For W32 systems this option is not required.

Please make sure that a proper pinentry program has been installed under the default filename (which is system dependent) or use the option 'pinentry-program' to specify the full name of that program. It is often useful to install a symbolic link from the actual used pinentry (e.g. '/usr/local/bin/pinentry-gtk') to the expected one (e.g. '/usr/local/bin/pinentry').

See [Option Index], page 167,for an index to GPG-AGENT's commands and options.

2.1 Commands

Commands are not distinguished from options except for the fact that only one command is allowed.

`--version`

Print the program version and licensing information. Note that you cannot abbreviate this command.

`--help`
`-h`

Print a usage message summarizing the most useful command-line options. Note that you cannot abbreviate this command.

`--dump-options`

Print a list of all available options and commands. Note that you cannot abbreviate this command.

`--server` Run in server mode and wait for commands on the `stdin`. The default mode is to create a socket and listen for commands there.

`--daemon [command line]`

Start the gpg-agent as a daemon; that is, detach it from the console and run it in the background.

As an alternative you may create a new process as a child of gpg-agent: `gpg-agent --daemon /bin/sh`. This way you get a new shell with the environment setup properly; after you exit from this shell, gpg-agent terminates within a few seconds.

2.2 Option Summary

`--options` *file*

> Reads configuration from *file* instead of from the default per-user configuration file. The default configuration file is named '`gpg-agent.conf`' and expected in the '`.gnupg`' directory directly below the home directory of the user.

`--homedir` *dir*

> Set the name of the home directory to *dir*. If this option is not used, the home directory defaults to '`~/.gnupg`'. It is only recognized when given on the command line. It also overrides any home directory stated through the environment variable `GNUPGHOME` or (on Windows systems) by means of the Registry entry *HKCU\Software\GNU\GnuPG:HomeDir*.

> On Windows systems it is possible to install GnuPG as a portable application. In this case only this command line option is considered, all other ways to set a home directory are ignored.

> To install GnuPG as a portable application under Windows, create an empty file name '`gpgconf.ctl`' in the same directory as the tool '`gpgconf.exe`'. The root of the installation is than that directory; or, if '`gpgconf.exe`' has been installed directly below a directory named '`bin`', its parent directory. You also need to make sure that the following directories exist and are writable: '`ROOT/home`' for the GnuPG home and '`ROOT/usr/local/var/cache/gnupg`' for internal cache files.

`-v`

`--verbose`

> Outputs additional information while running. You can increase the verbosity by giving several verbose commands to `gpgsm`, such as '`-vv`'.

`-q`

`--quiet`   Try to be as quiet as possible.

`--batch`   Don't invoke a pinentry or do any other thing requiring human interaction.

`--faked-system-time` *epoch*

> This option is only useful for testing; it sets the system time back or forth to *epoch* which is the number of seconds elapsed since the year 1970.

`--debug-level` *level*

> Select the debug level for investigating problems. *level* may be a numeric value or a keyword:

> > `none`   No debugging at all. A value of less than 1 may be used instead of the keyword.

> > `basic`   Some basic debug messages. A value between 1 and 2 may be used instead of the keyword.

> > `advanced` More verbose debug messages. A value between 3 and 5 may be used instead of the keyword.

expert   Even more detailed messages. A value between 6 and 8 may be used instead of the keyword.

guru   All of the debug messages you can get. A value greater than 8 may be used instead of the keyword. The creation of hash tracing files is only enabled if the keyword is used.

How these messages are mapped to the actual debugging flags is not specified and may change with newer releases of this program. They are however carefully selected to best aid in debugging.

`--debug` *flags*

This option is only useful for debugging and the behaviour may change at any time without notice. FLAGS are bit encoded and may be given in usual C-Syntax. The currently defined bits are:

0 (1)   X.509 or OpenPGP protocol related data

1 (2)   values of big number integers

2 (4)   low level crypto operations

5 (32)   memory allocation

6 (64)   caching

7 (128)   show memory statistics.

9 (512)   write hashed data to files named `dbgmd-000*`

10 (1024)   trace Assuan protocol

12 (4096)   bypass all certificate validation

`--debug-all`

Same as `--debug=0xffffffff`

`--debug-wait` *n*

When running in server mode, wait *n* seconds before entering the actual processing loop and print the pid. This gives time to attach a debugger.

`--debug-quick-random`

This option inhibits the use of the very secure random quality level (Libgcrypts `GCRY_VERY_STRONG_RANDOM`) and degrades all request down to standard random quality. It is only used for testing and shall not be used for any production quality keys. This option is only effective when given on the command line.

`--debug-pinentry`

This option enables extra debug information pertaining to the Pinentry. As of now it is only useful when used along with `--debug 1024`.

`--no-detach`

Don't detach the process from the console. This is mainly useful for debugging.

```
-s
--sh
-c
--csh     Format the info output in daemon mode for use with the standard Bourne shell
          or the C-shell respectively. The default is to guess it based on the environment
          variable SHELL which is correct in almost all cases.

--no-grab
          Tell the pinentry not to grab the keyboard and mouse. This option should in
          general not be used to avoid X-sniffing attacks.

--log-file file
          Append all logging output to file. This is very helpful in seeing
          what the agent actually does. If neither a log file nor a log file
          descriptor has been set on a Windows platform, the Registry entry
          HKCU\Software\GNU\GnuPG:DefaultLogFile, if set, is used to specify the
          logging output.

--no-allow-mark-trusted
          Do not allow clients to mark keys as trusted, i.e. put them into the
          'trustlist.txt' file. This makes it harder for users to inadvertently accept
          Root-CA keys.

--allow-preset-passphrase
          This option allows the use of gpg-preset-passphrase to seed the internal
          cache of gpg-agent with passphrases.

--allow-loopback-pinentry
          Allow clients to use the loopback pinentry features; see the option
          'pinentry-mode' for details.

--no-allow-external-cache
          Tell Pinentry not to enable features which use an external cache for passphrases.
          Some desktop environments prefer to unlock all credentials with one master
          password and may have installed a Pinentry which employs an additional ex-
          ternal cache to implement such a policy. By using this option the Pinentry is
          advised not to make use of such a cache and instead always ask the user for the
          requested passphrase.

--allow-emacs-pinentry
          Tell Pinentry to allow features to divert the passphrase entry to a running
          Emacs instance. How this is exactly handled depends on the version of the
          used Pinentry.

--ignore-cache-for-signing
          This option will let gpg-agent bypass the passphrase cache for all signing op-
          eration. Note that there is also a per-session option to control this behaviour
          but this command line option takes precedence.

--default-cache-ttl n
          Set the time a cache entry is valid to n seconds. The default is 600 seconds.
          Each time a cache entry is accessed, the entry's timer is reset. To set an entry's
          maximum lifetime, use max-cache-ttl.
```

`--default-cache-ttl-ssh n`

> Set the time a cache entry used for SSH keys is valid to n seconds. The default is 1800 seconds. Each time a cache entry is accessed, the entry's timer is reset. To set an entry's maximum lifetime, use `max-cache-ttl-ssh`.

`--max-cache-ttl n`

> Set the maximum time a cache entry is valid to n seconds. After this time a cache entry will be expired even if it has been accessed recently or has been set using `gpg-preset-passphrase`. The default is 2 hours (7200 seconds).

`--max-cache-ttl-ssh n`

> Set the maximum time a cache entry used for SSH keys is valid to n seconds. After this time a cache entry will be expired even if it has been accessed recently or has been set using `gpg-preset-passphrase`. The default is 2 hours (7200 seconds).

`--enforce-passphrase-constraints`

> Enforce the passphrase constraints by not allowing the user to bypass them using the "Take it anyway" button.

`--min-passphrase-len n`

> Set the minimal length of a passphrase. When entering a new passphrase shorter than this value a warning will be displayed. Defaults to 8.

`--min-passphrase-nonalpha n`

> Set the minimal number of digits or special characters required in a passphrase. When entering a new passphrase with less than this number of digits or special characters a warning will be displayed. Defaults to 1.

`--check-passphrase-pattern file`

> Check the passphrase against the pattern given in *file*. When entering a new passphrase matching one of these pattern a warning will be displayed. *file* should be an absolute filename. The default is not to use any pattern file.
>
> Security note: It is known that checking a passphrase against a list of pattern or even against a complete dictionary is not very effective to enforce good passphrases. Users will soon figure up ways to bypass such a policy. A better policy is to educate users on good security behavior and optionally to run a passphrase cracker regularly on all users passphrases to catch the very simple ones.

`--max-passphrase-days n`

> Ask the user to change the passphrase if n days have passed since the last change. With '`--enforce-passphrase-constraints`' set the user may not bypass this check.

`--enable-passphrase-history`

> This option does nothing yet.

`--pinentry-invisible-char char`

> This option asks the Pinentry to use *char* for displaying hidden characters. *char* must be one character UTF-8 string. A Pinentry may or may not honor this request.

`--pinentry-program` *filename*

> Use program *filename* as the PIN entry. The default is installation dependent. With the default configuration the name of the default pinentry is '`pinentry`'; if that file does not exist but a '`pinentry-basic`' exist the latter is used.
>
> On a Windows platform the default is to use the first existing program from this list: '`bin\pinentry.exe`', '`..\Gpg4win\bin\pinentry.exe`', '`..\Gpg4win\pinentry.exe`', '`..\GNU\GnuPG\pinentry.exe`', '`..\GNU\bin\pinentry.exe`', '`bin\pinentry-basic.exe`' where the file names are relative to the GnuPG installation directory.

`--pinentry-touch-file` *filename*

> By default the filename of the socket gpg-agent is listening for requests is passed to Pinentry, so that it can touch that file before exiting (it does this only in curses mode). This option changes the file passed to Pinentry to *filename*. The special name `/dev/null` may be used to completely disable this feature. Note that Pinentry will not create that file, it will only change the modification and access time.

`--scdaemon-program` *filename*

> Use program *filename* as the Smartcard daemon. The default is installation dependent and can be shown with the `gpgconf` command.

`--disable-scdaemon`

> Do not make use of the scdaemon tool. This option has the effect of disabling the ability to do smartcard operations. Note, that enabling this option at runtime does not kill an already forked scdaemon.

`--disable-check-own-socket`

> `gpg-agent` employs a periodic self-test to detect a stolen socket. This usually means a second instance of `gpg-agent` has taken over the socket and `gpg-agent` will then terminate itself. This option may be used to disable this self-test for debugging purposes.

`--use-standard-socket`
`--no-use-standard-socket`
`--use-standard-socket-p`

> Since GnuPG 2.1 the standard socket is always used. These options have no more effect. The command `gpg-agent --use-standard-socket-p` will thus always return success.

`--display` *string*
`--ttyname` *string*
`--ttytype` *string*
`--lc-ctype` *string*
`--lc-messages` *string*
`--xauthority` *string*

> These options are used with the server mode to pass localization information.

`--keep-tty`
`--keep-display`

> Ignore requests to change the current `tty` or X window system's `DISPLAY` variable respectively. This is useful to lock the pinentry to pop up at the `tty` or display you started the agent.

`--extra-socket name`

> Also listen on native gpg-agent connections on the given socket. The intended use for this extra socket is to setup a Unix domain socket forwarding from a remote machine to this socket on the local machine. A `gpg` running on the remote machine may then connect to the local gpg-agent and use its private keys. This allows to decrypt or sign data on a remote machine without exposing the private keys to the remote machine.

`--enable-ssh-support`
`--enable-putty-support`

> Enable the OpenSSH Agent protocol.
>
> In this mode of operation, the agent does not only implement the gpg-agent protocol, but also the agent protocol used by OpenSSH (through a separate socket). Consequently, it should be possible to use the gpg-agent as a drop-in replacement for the well known ssh-agent.
>
> SSH Keys, which are to be used through the agent, need to be added to the gpg-agent initially through the ssh-add utility. When a key is added, ssh-add will ask for the password of the provided key file and send the unprotected key material to the agent; this causes the gpg-agent to ask for a passphrase, which is to be used for encrypting the newly received key and storing it in a gpg-agent specific directory.
>
> Once a key has been added to the gpg-agent this way, the gpg-agent will be ready to use the key.
>
> Note: in case the gpg-agent receives a signature request, the user might need to be prompted for a passphrase, which is necessary for decrypting the stored key. Since the ssh-agent protocol does not contain a mechanism for telling the agent on which display/terminal it is running, gpg-agent's ssh-support will use the TTY or X display where gpg-agent has been started. To switch this display to the current one, the following command may be used:
>
>   gpg-connect-agent updatestartuptty /bye
>
> Although all GnuPG components try to start the gpg-agent as needed, this is not possible for the ssh support because ssh does not know about it. Thus if no GnuPG tool which accesses the agent has been run, there is no guarantee that ssh is able to use gpg-agent for authentication. To fix this you may start gpg-agent if needed using this simple command:
>
>   gpg-connect-agent /bye
>
> Adding the '`--verbose`' shows the progress of starting the agent.
>
> The '`--enable-putty-support`' is only available under Windows and allows the use of gpg-agent with the ssh implementation `putty`. This is similar to the regular ssh-agent support but makes use of Windows message queue as required by `putty`.

All the long options may also be given in the configuration file after stripping off the two leading dashes.

2.3 Configuration

There are a few configuration files needed for the operation of the agent. By default they may all be found in the current home directory (see [option –homedir], page 4).

'gpg-agent.conf'

> This is the standard configuration file read by gpg-agent on startup. It may contain any valid long option; the leading two dashes may not be entered and the option may not be abbreviated. This file is also read after a SIGHUP however only a few options will actually have an effect. This default name may be changed on the command line (see [option –options], page 4). You should backup this file.

'trustlist.txt'

> This is the list of trusted keys. You should backup this file.
>
> Comment lines, indicated by a leading hash mark, as well as empty lines are ignored. To mark a key as trusted you need to enter its fingerprint followed by a space and a capital letter S. Colons may optionally be used to separate the bytes of a fingerprint; this allows to cut and paste the fingerprint from a key listing output. If the line is prefixed with a ! the key is explicitly marked as not trusted.
>
> Here is an example where two keys are marked as ultimately trusted and one as not trusted:

```
# CN=Wurzel ZS 3,O=Intevation GmbH,C=DE
A6935DD34EF3087973C706FC311AA2CCF733765B S

# CN=PCA-1-Verwaltung-02/O=PKI-1-Verwaltung/C=DE
DC:BD:69:25:48:BD:BB:7E:31:6E:BB:80:D3:00:80:35:D4:F8:A6:CD S

# CN=Root-CA/O=Schlapphuete/L=Pullach/C=DE
!14:56:98:D3:FE:9C:CA:5A:31:6E:BC:81:D3:11:4E:00:90:A3:44:C2 S
```

> Before entering a key into this file, you need to ensure its authenticity. How to do this depends on your organisation; your administrator might have already entered those keys which are deemed trustworthy enough into this file. Places where to look for the fingerprint of a root certificate are letters received from the CA or the website of the CA (after making 100% sure that this is indeed the website of that CA). You may want to consider disallowing interactive updates of this file by using the See [option –no-allow-mark-trusted], page 6. It might even be advisable to change the permissions to read-only so that this file can't be changed inadvertently.
>
> As a special feature a line include-default will include a global list of trusted certificates (e.g. '/usr/local/etc/gnupg/trustlist.txt'). This global list is also used if the local list is not available.
>
> It is possible to add further flags after the S for use by the caller:

relax   Relax checking of some root certificate requirements. As of now this flag allows the use of root certificates with a missing basic-Constraints attribute (despite that it is a MUST for CA certificates) and disables CRL checking for the root certificate.

cm   If validation of a certificate finally issued by a CA with this flag set fails, try again using the chain validation model.

'sshcontrol'

This file is used when support for the secure shell agent protocol has been enabled (see [option --enable-ssh-support], page 9). Only keys present in this file are used in the SSH protocol. You should backup this file.

The **ssh-add** tool may be used to add new entries to this file; you may also add them manually. Comment lines, indicated by a leading hash mark, as well as empty lines are ignored. An entry starts with optional whitespace, followed by the keygrip of the key given as 40 hex digits, optionally followed by the caching TTL in seconds and another optional field for arbitrary flags. A non-zero TTL overrides the global default as set by '**--default-cache-ttl-ssh**'.

The only flag support is **confirm**. If this flag is found for a key, each use of the key will pop up a pinentry to confirm the use of that key. The flag is automatically set if a new key was loaded into **gpg-agent** using the option '**-c**' of the **ssh-add** command.

The keygrip may be prefixed with a ! to disable an entry entry.

The following example lists exactly one key. Note that keys available through a OpenPGP smartcard in the active smartcard reader are implicitly added to this list; i.e. there is no need to list them.

```
# Key added on: 2011-07-20 20:38:46
# Fingerprint:  5e:8d:c4:ad:e7:af:6e:27:8a:d6:13:e4:79:ad:0b:81
34B62F25E277CF13D3C6BCEBFD3F85D08F0A864B 0 confirm
```

'private-keys-v1.d/'

This is the directory where gpg-agent stores the private keys. Each key is stored in a file with the name made up of the keygrip and the suffix 'key'. You should backup all files in this directory and take great care to keep this backup closed away.

Note that on larger installations, it is useful to put predefined files into the directory '/usr/local/etc/skel/.gnupg' so that newly created users start up with a working configuration. For existing users the a small helper script is provided to create these files (see Section 8.3 [addgnupghome], page 117).

2.4 Use of some signals.

A running **gpg-agent** may be controlled by signals, i.e. using the **kill** command to send a signal to the process.

Here is a list of supported signals:

SIGHUP   This signal flushes all cached passphrases and if the program has been started
            with a configuration file, the configuration file is read again. Only certain
            options are honored: `quiet`, `verbose`, `debug`, `debug-all`, `debug-level`,
            `debug-pinentry`, `no-grab`, `pinentry-program`, `pinentry-invisible-char`,
            `default-cache-ttl`, `max-cache-ttl`, `ignore-cache-for-signing`, `no-`
            `allow-external-cache`, `allow-emacs-pinentry`, `no-allow-mark-trusted`,
            `disable-scdaemon`, and `disable-check-own-socket`. `scdaemon-program`
            is also supported but due to the current implementation, which calls the
            scdaemon only once, it is not of much use unless you manually kill the
            scdaemon.

SIGTERM   Shuts down the process but waits until all current requests are fulfilled. If the
            process has received 3 of these signals and requests are still pending, a shutdown
            is forced.

SIGINT   Shuts down the process immediately.

SIGUSR1   Dump internal information to the log file.

SIGUSR2   This signal is used for internal purposes.

2.5 Examples

It is important to set the GPG_TTY environment variable in your login shell, for example
in the '`~/.bashrc`' init script:

```
export GPG_TTY=$(tty)
```

If you enabled the Ssh Agent Support, you also need to tell ssh about it by adding this
to your init script:

```
unset SSH_AGENT_PID
if [ "${gnupg_SSH_AUTH_SOCK_by:-0}" -ne $$ ]; then
  export SSH_AUTH_SOCK="${HOME}/.gnupg/S.gpg-agent.ssh"
fi
```

2.6 Agent's Assuan Protocol

Note: this section does only document the protocol, which is used by GnuPG components;
it does not deal with the ssh-agent protocol.

The **gpg-agent** daemon is started on demand by the GnuPG components.

To identify a key we use a thing called keygrip which is the SHA-1 hash of an canonical
encoded S-Expression of the public key as used in Libgcrypt. For the purpose of this
interface the keygrip is given as a hex string. The advantage of using this and not the hash
of a certificate is that it will be possible to use the same keypair for different protocols,
thereby saving space on the token used to keep the secret keys.

The **gpg-agent** may send status messages during a command or when returning from
a command to inform a client about the progress or result of an operation. For example,

the *INQUIRE_MAXLEN* status message may be sent during a server inquire to inform the client of the maximum usable length of the inquired data (which should not be exceeded).

2.6.1 Decrypting a session key

The client asks the server to decrypt a session key. The encrypted session key should have all information needed to select the appropriate secret key or to delegate it to a smartcard.

        SETKEY <keyGrip>

Tell the server about the key to be used for decryption. If this is not used, `gpg-agent` may try to figure out the key by trying to decrypt the message with each key available.

        PKDECRYPT

The agent checks whether this command is allowed and then does an INQUIRY to get the ciphertext the client should then send the cipher text.

        S: INQUIRE CIPHERTEXT
        C: D (xxxxxx
        C: D xxxx)
        C: END

Please note that the server may send status info lines while reading the data lines from the client. The data send is a SPKI like S-Exp with this structure:

        (enc-val
          (<algo>
            (<param_name1> <mpi>)
        ...
            (<param_namen> <mpi>)))

Where algo is a string with the name of the algorithm; see the libgcrypt documentation for a list of valid algorithms. The number and names of the parameters depend on the algorithm. The agent does return an error if there is an inconsistency.

If the decryption was successful the decrypted data is returned by means of "D" lines.

Here is an example session:

```
C: PKDECRYPT
S: INQUIRE CIPHERTEXT
C: D (enc-val elg (a 349324324)
C: D    (b 3F444677CA)))
C: END
S: # session key follows
S: S PADDING 0
S: D (value 1234567890ABCDEF0)
S: OK descryption successful
```

The PADDING status line is only send if gpg-agent can tell what kind of padding is used. As of now only the value 0 is used to indicate that the padding has been removed.

2.6.2 Signing a Hash

The client ask the agent to sign a given hash value. A default key will be chosen if no key has been set. To set a key a client first uses:

```
SIGKEY <keyGrip>
```

This can be used multiple times to create multiple signature, the list of keys is reset with the next PKSIGN command or a RESET. The server test whether the key is a valid key to sign something and responds with okay.

```
SETHASH --hash=<name>|<algo> <hexstring>
```

The client can use this command to tell the server about the data <hexstring> (which usually is a hash) to be signed. <algo> is the decimal encoded hash algorithm number as used by Libgcrypt. Either <algo> or –hash=<name> must be given. Valid names for <name> are:

`sha1`   The SHA-1 hash algorithm

`sha256`   The SHA-256 hash algorithm

`rmd160`   The RIPE-MD160 hash algorithm

`md5`   The old and broken MD5 hash algorithm

`tls-md5sha1`
            A combined hash algorithm as used by the TLS protocol.

The actual signing is done using

```
PKSIGN <options>
```

Options are not yet defined, but my later be used to choose among different algorithms. The agent does then some checks, asks for the passphrase and as a result the server returns the signature as an SPKI like S-expression in "D" lines:

```
(sig-val
  (<algo>
    (<param_name1> <mpi>)
  ...
    (<param_namen> <mpi>)))
```

The operation is affected by the option

```
OPTION use-cache-for-signing=0|1
```

The default of 1 uses the cache. Setting this option to 0 will lead **gpg-agent** to ignore the passphrase cache. Note, that there is also a global command line option for **gpg-agent** to globally disable the caching.

Here is an example session:

```
C: SIGKEY <keyGrip>
S: OK key available
C: SIGKEY <keyGrip>
S: OK key available
C: PKSIGN
S: # I did ask the user whether he really wants to sign
S: # I did ask the user for the passphrase
S: INQUIRE HASHVAL
C: D ABCDEF012345678901234
C: END
S: # signature follows
S: D (sig-val rsa (s 45435453654612121212))
S: OK
```

2.6.3 Generating a Key

This is used to create a new keypair and store the secret key inside the active PSE — which is in most cases a Soft-PSE. An not yet defined option allows to choose the storage location. To get the secret key out of the PSE, a special export tool has to be used.

        GENKEY [--no-protection] [--preset] [<cache_nonce>]

Invokes the key generation process and the server will then inquire on the generation parameters, like:

```
S: INQUIRE KEYPARM
C: D (genkey (rsa (nbits  1024)))
C: END
```

The format of the key parameters which depends on the algorithm is of the form:

```
(genkey
  (algo
    (parameter_name_1 ....)
        ....
    (parameter_name_n ....)))
```

If everything succeeds, the server returns the *public key* in a SPKI like S-Expression like this:

```
(public-key
   (rsa
(n <mpi>)
(e <mpi>)))
```

Here is an example session:

```
C: GENKEY
S: INQUIRE KEYPARM
C: D (genkey (rsa (nbits  1024)))
C: END
S: D (public-key
S: D   (rsa (n 326487324683264) (e 10001)))
S  OK key created
```

The '--no-protection' option may be used to prevent prompting for a passphrase to protect the secret key while leaving the secret key unprotected. The '--preset' option may be used to add the passphrase to the cache using the default cache parameters.

The '--inq-passwd' option may be used to create the key with a supplied passphrase. When used the agent does an inquiry with the keyword NEWPASSWD to retrieve that passphrase. This option takes precedence over '--no-protection'; however if the client sends a empty (zero-length) passphrase, this is identical to '--no-protection'.

2.6.4 Importing a Secret Key

This operation is not yet supported by GpgAgent. Specialized tools are to be used for this.

There is no actual need because we can expect that secret keys created by a 3rd party are stored on a smartcard. If we have generated the key ourself, we do not need to import it.

2.6.5 Export a Secret Key

Not implemented.

Should be done by an extra tool.

2.6.6 Importing a Root Certificate

Actually we do not import a Root Cert but provide a way to validate any piece of data by storing its Hash along with a description and an identifier in the PSE. Here is the interface description:

```
ISTRUSTED <fingerprint>
```

Check whether the OpenPGP primary key or the X.509 certificate with the given fingerprint is an ultimately trusted key or a trusted Root CA certificate. The fingerprint should be given as a hexstring (without any blanks or colons or whatever in between) and may be left padded with 00 in case of an MD5 fingerprint. GPGAgent will answer with:

```
OK
```

The key is in the table of trusted keys.

```
ERR 304 (Not Trusted)
```

The key is not in this table.

Gpg needs the entire list of trusted keys to maintain the web of trust; the following command is therefore quite helpful:

```
LISTTRUSTED
```

GpgAgent returns a list of trusted keys line by line:

```
S: D 000000001234454556565656677878AF2F1ECCFF P
S: D 3403875634856348564356456348564385764457A P
S: D FEDC6532453745367FD83474357495743757435D S
S: OK
```

The first item on a line is the hexified fingerprint where MD5 fingerprints are 00 padded to the left and the second item is a flag to indicate the type of key (so that gpg is able to only take care of PGP keys). P = OpenPGP, S = S/MIME. A client should ignore the rest of the line, so that we can extend the format in the future.

Finally a client should be able to mark a key as trusted:

```
MARKTRUSTED fingerprint "P"|"S"
```

The server will then pop up a window to ask the user whether she really trusts this key. For this it will probably ask for a text to be displayed like this:

```
S: INQUIRE TRUSTDESC
C: D Do you trust the key with the fingerprint @FPR@
C: D bla fasel blurb.
C: END
S: OK
```

Known sequences with the pattern @foo@ are replaced according to this table:

@FPR16@   Format the fingerprint according to gpg rules for a v3 keys.

@FPR20@   Format the fingerprint according to gpg rules for a v4 keys.

@FPR@   Choose an appropriate format to format the fingerprint.

@@   Replaced by a single @

2.6.7 Ask for a passphrase

This function is usually used to ask for a passphrase to be used for symmetric encryption, but may also be used by programs which need special handling of passphrases. This command uses a syntax which helps clients to use the agent with minimum effort.

```
GET_PASSPHRASE [--data] [--check] [--no-ask] [--repeat[=N]] \
               [--qualitybar] cache_id                    \
               [error_message prompt description]
```

cache_id is expected to be a string used to identify a cached passphrase. Use a X to bypass the cache. With no other arguments the agent returns a cached passphrase or an error. By convention either the hexified fingerprint of the key shall be used for *cache_id* or an arbitrary string prefixed with the name of the calling application and a colon: Like `gpg:somestring`.

error_message is either a single X for no error message or a string to be shown as an error message like (e.g. "invalid passphrase"). Blanks must be percent escaped or replaced by +'.

prompt is either a single X for a default prompt or the text to be shown as the prompt. Blanks must be percent escaped or replaced by +.

description is a text shown above the entry field. Blanks must be percent escaped or replaced by +.

The agent either returns with an error or with a OK followed by the hex encoded passphrase. Note that the length of the strings is implicitly limited by the maximum length of a command. If the option '--data' is used, the passphrase is not returned on the OK line but by regular data lines; this is the preferred method.

If the option '--check' is used, the standard passphrase constraints checks are applied. A check is not done if the passphrase has been found in the cache.

If the option '--no-ask' is used and the passphrase is not in the cache the user will not be asked to enter a passphrase but the error code `GPG_ERR_NO_DATA` is returned.

If the option '--qualitybar' is used and a minimum passphrase length has been configured, a visual indication of the entered passphrase quality is shown.

```
CLEAR_PASSPHRASE cache_id
```

may be used to invalidate the cache entry for a passphrase. The function returns with OK even when there is no cached passphrase.

2.6.8 Remove a cached passphrase

Use this command to remove a cached passphrase.

```
CLEAR_PASSPHRASE [--mode=normal] <cache_id>
```

The '--mode=normal' option can be used to clear a *cache_id* that was set by gpg-agent.

2.6.9 Set a passphrase for a keygrip

This command adds a passphrase to the cache for the specified *keygrip*.

```
PRESET_PASSPHRASE [--inquire] <string_or_keygrip> <timeout> [<hexstring>]
```

The passphrase is a hexidecimal string when specified. When not specified, the passphrase will be retrieved from the pinentry module unless the '--inquire' option was specified in which case the passphrase will be retrieved from the client.

The *timeout* parameter keeps the passphrase cached for the specified number of seconds. A value of -1 means infinate while 0 means the default (currently only a timeout of -1 is allowed, which means to never expire it).

2.6.10 Ask for confirmation

This command may be used to ask for a simple confirmation by presenting a text and 2 buttons: Okay and Cancel.

```
GET_CONFIRMATION description
```

*description*is displayed along with a Okay and Cancel button. Blanks must be percent escaped or replaced by +. A X may be used to display confirmation dialog with a default text.

The agent either returns with an error or with a OK. Note, that the length of *description* is implicitly limited by the maximum length of a command.

2.6.11 Check whether a key is available

This can be used to see whether a secret key is available. It does not return any information on whether the key is somehow protected.

```
HAVEKEY keygrips
```

The agent answers either with OK or No_Secret_Key (208). The caller may want to check for other error codes as well. More than one keygrip may be given. In this case the command returns success if at least one of the keygrips corresponds to an available secret key.

2.6.12 Register a smartcard

```
LEARN [--send]
```

This command is used to register a smartcard. With the –send option given the certificates are send back.

2.6.13 Change a Passphrase

```
PASSWD [--cache-nonce=<c>] [--passwd-nonce=<s>] [--preset] keygrip
```

This command is used to interactively change the passphrase of the key identified by the hex string *keygrip*. The '--preset' option may be used to add the new passphrase to the cache using the default cache parameters.

2.6.14 Change the standard display

```
UPDATESTARTUPTTY
```

Set the startup TTY and X-DISPLAY variables to the values of this session. This command is useful to direct future pinentry invocations to another screen. It is only required because there is no way in the ssh-agent protocol to convey this information.

2.6.15 Get the Event Counters

`GETEVENTCOUNTER`

This function return one status line with the current values of the event counters. The event counters are useful to avoid polling by delaying a poll until something has changed. The values are decimal numbers in the range 0 to `UINT_MAX` and wrapping around to 0. The actual values should not be relied upon; they shall only be used to detect a change.

The currently defined counters are are:

ANY   Incremented with any change of any of the other counters.

KEY   Incremented for added or removed private keys.

CARD   Incremented for changes of the card readers stati.

2.6.16 Return information about the process

This is a multipurpose function to return a variety of information.

`GETINFO what`

The value of *what* specifies the kind of information returned:

version   Return the version of the program.

pid   Return the process id of the process.

socket_name
            Return the name of the socket used to connect the agent.

ssh_socket_name
            Return the name of the socket used for SSH connections. If SSH support has not been enabled the error `GPG_ERR_NO_DATA` will be returned.

2.6.17 Set options for the session

Here is a list of session options which are not yet described with other commands. The general syntax for an Assuan option is:

`OPTION key=value`

Supported *keys* are:

agent-awareness
            This may be used to tell gpg-agent of which gpg-agent version the client is aware of. gpg-agent uses this information to enable features which might break older clients.

putenv   Change the session's environment to be used for the Pinentry. Valid values are:

            name   Delete envvar *name*

            name=   Set envvar *name* to the empty string

            name=value Set envvar *name* to the string *value*.

`use-cache-for-signing`
>   See Assuan command `PKSIGN`.

`allow-pinentry-notify`
>   This does not need any value. It is used to enable the PINENTRY_LAUNCHED inquiry.

`pinentry-mode`
>   This option is used to change the operation mode of the pinentry. The following values are defined:

>   `ask`   This is the default mode which pops up a pinentry as needed.

>   `cancel`   Instead of popping up a pinentry, return the error code `GPG_ERR_CANCELED`.

>   `error`   Instead of popping up a pinentry, return the error code `GPG_ERR_NO_PIN_ENTRY`.

>   `loopback`   Use a loopback pinentry. This fakes a pinentry by using inquiries back to the caller to ask for a passphrase. This option may only be set if the agent has been configured for that. Use the See [option –allow-loopback-pinentry], page 6.

`cache-ttl-opt-preset`
>   This option sets the cache TTL for new entries created by GENKEY and PASSWD commands when using the '`--preset`' option. It it is not used a default value is used.

`s2k-count`

>   Instead of using the standard S2K count (which is computed on the fly), the given S2K count is used for new keys or when changing the passphrase of a key. Values below 65536 are considered to be 0. This option is valid for the entire session or until reset to 0. This option is useful if the key is later used on boxes which are either much slower or faster than the actual box.

3 Invoking DIRMNGR

Since version 2.1 of GnuPG, `dirmngr` takes care of accessing the OpenPGP keyservers. As with previous versions it is also used as a server for managing and downloading certificate revocation lists (CRLs) for X.509 certificates, downloading X.509 certificates, and providing access to OCSP providers. Dirmngr is invoked internally by `gpg`, `gpgsm`, or via the `gpg-connect-agent` tool.

For historical reasons it is also possible to start `dirmngr` in a system daemon mode which uses a different directory layout. However, this mode is deprecated and may eventually be removed.

See [Option Index], page 167, for an index to DIRMNGR's commands and options.

3.1 Commands

Commands are not distinguished from options except for the fact that only one command is allowed.

`--version`

> Print the program version and licensing information. Note that you cannot abbreviate this command.

`--help, -h`

> Print a usage message summarizing the most useful command-line options. Not that you cannot abbreviate this command.

`--dump-options`

> Print a list of all available options and commands. Note that you cannot abbreviate this command.

`--server`   Run in server mode and wait for commands on the **stdin**. The default mode is to create a socket and listen for commands there. This is only used for testing.

`--daemon`   Run in background daemon mode and listen for commands on a socket. Note that this also changes the default home directory and enables the internal certificate validation code. This mode is deprecated.

`--list-crls`

> List the contents of the CRL cache on **stdout**. This is probably only useful for debugging purposes.

`--load-crl` *file*

> This command requires a filename as additional argument, and it will make Dirmngr try to import the CRL in *file* into it's cache. Note, that this is only possible if Dirmngr is able to retrieve the CA's certificate directly by its own means. In general it is better to use **gpgsm**'s `--call-dirmngr loadcrl filename` command so that **gpgsm** can help dirmngr.

`--fetch-crl` *url*

> This command requires an URL as additional argument, and it will make dirmngr try to retrieve an import the CRL from that *url* into it's cache. This is mainly useful for debugging purposes. The **dirmngr-client** provides the same feature for a running dirmngr.

`--shutdown`

> This commands shuts down an running instance of Dirmngr. This command has currently no effect.

`--flush`   This command removes all CRLs from Dirmngr's cache. Client requests will thus trigger reading of fresh CRLs.

3.2 Option Summary

`--options` *file*

> Reads configuration from *file* instead of from the default per-user configuration file. The default configuration file is named '`dirmngr.conf`' and expected in the home directory.

`--homedir` *dir*

> Set the name of the home directory to *dir*. This option is only effective when used on the command line. The default depends on the running mode:

> With `--daemon` given on the commandline
> > the directory named '`/usr/local/etc/gnupg`' is used for configuration files and '`/usr/local/var/cache/gnupg`' for cached CRLs.

> Without `--daemon` given on the commandline
> > the directory named '`.gnupg`' directly below the home directory of the user unless the environment variable `GNUPGHOME` has been set in which case its value will be used. All kind of data is stored below this directory.

`-v`

`--verbose`

> Outputs additional information while running. You can increase the verbosity by giving several verbose commands to DIRMNGR, such as '`-vv`'.

`--log-file` *file*

> Append all logging output to *file*. This is very helpful in seeing what the agent actually does.

`--debug-level` *level*

> Select the debug level for investigating problems. *level* may be a numeric value or by a keyword:

> `none`   No debugging at all. A value of less than 1 may be used instead of the keyword.

> `basic`   Some basic debug messages. A value between 1 and 2 may be used instead of the keyword.

> `advanced` More verbose debug messages. A value between 3 and 5 may be used instead of the keyword.

> `expert`   Even more detailed messages. A value between 6 and 8 may be used instead of the keyword.

guru   All of the debug messages you can get. A value greater than 8 may be used instead of the keyword. The creation of hash tracing files is only enabled if the keyword is used.

How these messages are mapped to the actual debugging flags is not specified and may change with newer releases of this program. They are however carefully selected to best aid in debugging.

--debug *flags*

This option is only useful for debugging and the behaviour may change at any time without notice. FLAGS are bit encoded and may be given in usual C-Syntax.

--debug-all

Same as --debug=0xffffffff

--gnutls-debug *level*

Enable debugging of GNUTLS at *level*.

--debug-wait *n*

When running in server mode, wait *n* seconds before entering the actual processing loop and print the pid. This gives time to attach a debugger.

-s
--sh
-c
--csh   Format the info output in daemon mode for use with the standard Bourne shell respective the C-shell . The default ist to guess it based on the environment variable SHELL which is in almost all cases sufficient.

--force   Enabling this option forces loading of expired CRLs; this is only useful for debugging.

--use-tor

This options is not yet functional! It will eventually switch GnuPG into a TOR mode to route all network access via TOR (an anonymity network).

--keyserver name

Use **name** as your keyserver. This is the server that **gpg** communicates with to receive keys, send keys, and search for keys. The format of the **name** is a URI: 'scheme:[//]keyservername[:port]' The scheme is the type of keyserver: "hkp" for the HTTP (or compatible) keyservers, "ldap" for the LDAP keyservers, or "mailto" for the Graff email keyserver. Note that your particular installation of GnuPG may have other keyserver types available as well. Keyserver schemes are case-insensitive. After the keyserver name, optional keyserver configuration options may be provided. These are the same as the global '**--keyserver-options**' from below, but apply only to this particular keyserver.

Most keyservers synchronize with each other, so there is generally no need to send keys to more than one server. The keyserver hkp://keys.gnupg.net uses round robin DNS to give a different keyserver each time you use it.

--disable-ldap

Entirely disables the use of LDAP.

`--disable-http`
>   Entirely disables the use of HTTP.

`--ignore-http-dp`
>   When looking for the location of a CRL, the to be tested certificate usually contains so called *CRL Distribution Point* (DP) entries which are URLs describing the way to access the CRL. The first found DP entry is used. With this option all entries using the HTTP scheme are ignored when looking for a suitable DP.

`--ignore-ldap-dp`
>   This is similar to '`--ignore-http-dp`' but ignores entries using the LDAP scheme. Both options may be combined resulting in ignoring DPs entirely.

`--ignore-ocsp-service-url`
>   Ignore all OCSP URLs contained in the certificate. The effect is to force the use of the default responder.

`--honor-http-proxy`
>   If the environment variable `http_proxy` has been set, use its value to access HTTP servers.

`--http-proxy host[:port]`
>   Use *host* and *port* to access HTTP servers. The use of this option overrides the environment variable `http_proxy` regardless whether '`--honor-http-proxy`' has been set.

`--ldap-proxy host[:port]`
>   Use *host* and *port* to connect to LDAP servers. If *port* is ommitted, port 389 (standard LDAP port) is used. This overrides any specified host and port part in a LDAP URL and will also be used if host and port have been ommitted from the URL.

`--only-ldap-proxy`
>   Never use anything else but the LDAP "proxy" as configured with '`--ldap-proxy`'. Usually `dirmngr` tries to use other configured LDAP server if the connection using the "proxy" failed.

`--ldapserverlist-file file`
>   Read the list of LDAP servers to consult for CRLs and certificates from file instead of the default per-user ldap server list file. The default value for *file* is '`dirmngr_ldapservers.conf`' or '`ldapservers.conf`' when running in '`--daemon`' mode.
>
>   This server list file contains one LDAP server per line in the format
>
>   HOSTNAME:PORT:USERNAME:PASSWORD:BASE_DN
>
>   Lines starting with a '`#`' are comments.
>
>   Note that as usual all strings entered are expected to be UTF-8 encoded. Obviously this will lead to problems if the password has orginally been encoded as Latin-1. There is no other solution here than to put such a password in the binary encoding into the file (i.e. non-ascii characters won't show up readable).[1]

---

[1] The `gpgconf` tool might be helpful for frontends as it allows to edit this configuration file using percent escaped strings.

`--ldaptimeout` *secs*

>   Specify the number of seconds to wait for an LDAP query before timing out. The default is currently 100 seconds. 0 will never timeout.

`--add-servers`

>   This options makes dirmngr add any servers it discovers when validating certificates against CRLs to the internal list of servers to consult for certificates and CRLs.

>   This options is useful when trying to validate a certificate that has a CRL distribution point that points to a server that is not already listed in the ldapserverlist. Dirmngr will always go to this server and try to download the CRL, but chances are high that the certificate used to sign the CRL is located on the same server. So if dirmngr doesn't add that new server to list, it will often not be able to verify the signature of the CRL unless the `--add-servers` option is used.

>   Note: The current version of dirmngr has this option disabled by default.

`--allow-ocsp`

>   This option enables OCSP support if requested by the client.

>   OCSP requests are rejected by default because they may violate the privacy of the user; for example it is possible to track the time when a user is reading a mail.

`--ocsp-responder` *url*

>   Use *url* as the default OCSP Responder if the certificate does not contain information about an assigned responder. Note, that `--ocsp-signer` must also be set to a valid certificate.

`--ocsp-signer` *fpr|file*

>   Use the certificate with the fingerprint *fpr* to check the responses of the default OCSP Responder. Alternativly a filename can be given in which case the respinse is expected to be signed by one of the certificates described in that file. Any argument which contains a slash, dot or tilde is considered a filename. Usual filename expansion takes place: A tilde at the start followed by a slash is replaced by the content of `HOME`, no slash at start describes a relative filename which will be searched at the home directory. To make sure that the *file* is searched in the home directory, either prepend the name with "./" or use a name which contains a dot.

>   If a response has been signed by a certificate described by these fingerprints no further check upon the validity of this certificate is done.

>   The format of the *FILE* is a list of SHA-1 fingerprint, one per line with optional colons between the bytes. Empty lines and lines prefix with a hash mark are ignored.

`--ocsp-max-clock-skew` *n*

>   The number of seconds a skew between the OCSP responder and them local clock is accepted. Default is 600 (20 minutes).

`--ocsp-max-period` *n*

> Seconds a response is at maximum considered valid after the time given in the thisUpdate field. Default is 7776000 (90 days).

`--ocsp-current-period` *n*

> The number of seconds an OCSP response is considered valid after the time given in the NEXT_UPDATE datum. Default is 10800 (3 hours).

`--max-replies` *n*

> Do not return more that *n* items in one query. The default is 10.

`--ignore-cert-extension` *oid*

> Add *oid* to the list of ignored certificate extensions. The *oid* is expected to be in dotted decimal form, like `2.5.29.3`. This option may be used more than once. Critical flagged certificate extensions matching one of the OIDs in the list are treated as if they are actually handled and thus the certificate won't be rejected due to an unknown critical extension. Use this option with care because extensions are usually flagged as critical for a reason.

`--hkp-cacert` *file*

> Use the root certificates in *file* for verification of the TLS certificates used with `hkps` (keyserver access over TLS). If the file is in PEM format a suffix of `.pem` is expected for *file*. This option may be given multiple times to add more root certificates. Tilde expansion is supported.

3.3 Configuration

Dirmngr makes use of several directories when running in daemon mode:

'`~/.gnupg`'
'`/etc/gnupg`'

> The first is the standard home directory for all configuration files. In the deprecated system daemon mode the second directory is used instead.

'`/etc/gnupg/trusted-certs`'

> This directory should be filled with certificates of Root CAs you are trusting in checking the CRLs and signing OCSP Reponses.

> Usually these are the same certificates you use with the applications making use of dirmngr. It is expected that each of these certificate files contain exactly one DER encoded certificate in a file with the suffix '`.crt`' or '`.der`'. `dirmngr` reads those certificates on startup and when given a SIGHUP. Certificates which are not readable or do not make up a proper X.509 certificate are ignored; see the log file for details.

> Applications using dirmngr (e.g. gpgsm) can request these certificates to complete a trust chain in the same way as with the extra-certs directory (see below).

> Note that for OCSP responses the certificate specified using the option '`--ocsp-signer`' is always considered valid to sign OCSP requests.

'`/etc/gnupg/extra-certs`'

> This directory may contain extra certificates which are preloaded into the interal cache on startup. Applications using dirmngr (e.g. gpgsm) can request cached

certificates to complete a trust chain. This is convenient in cases you have a couple intermediate CA certificates or certificates ususally used to sign OCSP reponses. These certificates are first tried before going out to the net to look for them. These certificates must also be DER encoded and suffixed with '.crt' or '.der'.

'/usr/local/var/run/gnupg'

> This directory is only uscd in the deprecated system daemon mode. It keeps the socket file for accessing dirmngr services. The name of the socket file will be 'S.dirmngr'. Make sure that this directory has the proper permissions to let dirmngr create the socket file and that eligible users may read and write to that socket.

'~/.gnupg/crls.d'
'/usr/local/var/cache/gnupg/crls.d'

> The first directory is used to store cached CRLs. The 'crls.d' part will be created by dirmngr if it does not exists but you need to make sure that the upper directory exists. The second directory is used instead in the deprecated systems daemon mode.

To be able to see what's going on you should create the configure file '~/gnupg/dirmngr.conf' with at least one line:

    log-file ~/dirmngr.log

To be able to perform OCSP requests you probably want to add the line:

    allow-ocsp

To make sure that new options are read and that after the installation of a new GnuPG versions the installed dirmngr is running, you may want to kill an existing dirmngr first:

    gpgconf --kill dirmngr

You may check the log file to see whether all desired root certificates have been loaded correctly.

3.4 Use of signals.

A running dirmngr may be controlled by signals, i.e. using the kill command to send a signal to the process.

Here is a list of supported signals:

SIGHUP   This signals flushes all internally cached CRLs as well as any cached certificates. Then the certificate cache is reinitialized as on startup. Options are re-read from the configuration file. Instead of sending this signal it is better to use

          gpgconf --reload dirmngr

SIGTERM   Shuts down the process but waits until all current requests are fulfilled. If the process has received 3 of these signals and requests are still pending, a shutdown is forced. You may also use

          gpgconf --kill dirmngr

          instead of this signal

SIGINT   Shuts down the process immediately.

SIGUSR1   This prints some caching statistics to the log file.

3.5 Examples

Here is an example on how to show dirmngr's internal table of OpenPGP keyserver addresses. The output is intended for debugging purposes and not part of a defined API.

```
gpg-connect-agent --dirmngr 'keyserver --hosttable' /bye
```

To inhibit the use of a particular host you have noticed in one of the keyserver pools, you may use

```
gpg-connect-agent --dirmngr 'keyserver --dead pgpkeys.bnd.de' /bye
```

The description of the `keyserver` command can be printed using

```
gpg-connect-agent --dirmngr 'help keyserver' /bye
```

3.6 Dirmngr's Assuan Protocol

Assuan is the IPC protocol used to access dirmngr. This is a description of the commands implemented by dirmngr.

3.6.1 Return the certificate(s) found

Lookup certificate. To allow multiple patterns (which are ORed) quoting is required: Spaces are to be translated into "+" or into "%20"; obviously this requires that the usual escape quoting rules are applied. The server responds with:

```
S: D <DER encoded certificate>
S: END
S: D <second DER encoded certificate>
S: END
S: OK
```

In this example 2 certificates are returned. The server may return any number of certificates; OK will also be returned when no certificates were found. The dirmngr might return a status line

```
S: S TRUNCATED <n>
```

To indicate that the output was truncated to N items due to a limitation of the server or by an arbitrary set limit.

The option '`--url`' may be used if instead of a search pattern a complete URL to the certificate is known:

```
C: LOOKUP --url CN%3DWerner%20Koch,o%3DIntevation%20GmbH,c%3DDE?userCertificate
```

If the option '`--cache-only`' is given, no external lookup is done so that only certificates from the cache are returned.

With the option '`--single`', the first and only the first match will be returned. Unless option '`--cache-only`' is also used, no local lookup will be done in this case.

3.6.2 Validate a certificate using a CRL or OCSP

```
ISVALID [--only-ocsp] [--force-default-responder] certid|certfpr
```

Check whether the certificate described by the *certid* has been revoked. Due to caching, the Dirmngr is able to answer immediately in most cases.

The *certid* is a hex encoded string consisting of two parts, delimited by a single dot. The first part is the SHA-1 hash of the issuer name and the second part the serial number.

Alternatively the certificate's SHA-1 fingerprint *certfpr* may be given in which case an OCSP request is done before consulting the CRL. If the option '--only-ocsp' is given, no fallback to a CRL check will be used. If the option '--force-default-responder' is given, only the default OCSP responder will be used and any other methods of obtaining an OCSP responder URL won't be used.

Common return values are:

GPG_ERR_NO_ERROR (0)
> This is the positive answer: The certificate is not revoked and we have an up-to-date revocation list for that certificate. If OCSP was used the responder confirmed that the certificate has not been revoked.

GPG_ERR_CERT_REVOKED
> This is the negative answer: The certificate has been revoked. Either it is in a CRL and that list is up to date or an OCSP responder informed us that it has been revoked.

GPG_ERR_NO_CRL_KNOWN
> No CRL is known for this certificate or the CRL is not valid or out of date.

GPG_ERR_NO_DATA
> The OCSP responder returned an "unknown" status. This means that it is not aware of the certificate's status.

GPG_ERR_NOT_SUPPORTED
> This is commonly seen if OCSP support has not been enabled in the configuration.

If DirMngr has not enough information about the given certificate (which is the case for not yet cached certificates), it will will inquire the missing data:

```
S: INQUIRE SENDCERT <CertID>
C: D <DER encoded certificate>
C: END
```

A client should be aware that DirMngr may ask for more than one certificate.

If Dirmngr has a certificate but the signature of the certificate could not been validated because the root certificate is not known to dirmngr as trusted, it may ask back to see whether the client trusts this the root certificate:

```
S: INQUIRE ISTRUSTED <CertHexfpr>
C: D 1
C: END
```

Only this answer will let Dirmngr consider the CRL as valid.

3.6.3 Validate a certificate using a CRL

Check whether the certificate with FINGERPRINT (SHA-1 hash of the entire X.509 certificate blob) is valid or not by consulting the CRL responsible for this certificate. If the fingerprint has not been given or the certificate is not know, the function inquires the certificate using:

```
S: INQUIRE TARGETCERT
C: D <DER encoded certificate>
C: END
```

Thus the caller is expected to return the certificate for the request (which should match FINGERPRINT) as a binary blob. Processing then takes place without further interaction; in particular dirmngr tries to locate other required certificate by its own mechanism which includes a local certificate store as well as a list of trusted root certificates.

The return code is 0 for success; i.e. the certificate has not been revoked or one of the usual error codes from libgpg-error.

3.6.4 Validate a certificate using OCSP

```
CHECKOCSP [--force-default-responder] [fingerprint]
```

Check whether the certificate with *fingerprint* (the SHA-1 hash of the entire X.509 certificate blob) is valid by consulting the appropiate OCSP responder. If the fingerprint has not been given or the certificate is not known by Dirmngr, the function inquires the certificate using:

```
S: INQUIRE TARGETCERT
C: D <DER encoded certificate>
C: END
```

Thus the caller is expected to return the certificate for the request (which should match *fingerprint*) as a binary blob. Processing then takes place without further interaction; in particular dirmngr tries to locate other required certificates by its own mechanism which includes a local certificate store as well as a list of trusted root certificates.

If the option '--force-default-responder' is given, only the default OCSP responder is used. This option is the per-command variant of the global option '--ignore-ocsp-service-url'.

The return code is 0 for success; i.e. the certificate has not been revoked or one of the usual error codes from libgpg-error.

3.6.5 Put a certificate into the internal cache

Put a certificate into the internal cache. This command might be useful if a client knows in advance certificates required for a test and wnats to make sure they get added to the internal cache. It is also helpful for debugging. To get the actual certificate, this command immediately inquires it using

```
S: INQUIRE TARGETCERT
C: D <DER encoded certificate>
C: END
```

Thus the caller is expected to return the certificate for the request as a binary blob.

The return code is 0 for success; i.e. the certificate has not been succesfully cached or one of the usual error codes from libgpg-error.

3.6.6 Validate a certificate for debugging

Validate a certificate using the certificate validation function used internally by dirmngr. This command is only useful for debugging. To get the actual certificate, this command immediately inquires it using

```
S: INQUIRE TARGETCERT
C: D <DER encoded certificate>
C: END
```

Thus the caller is expected to return the certificate for the request as a binary blob.

4 Invoking GPG

`gpg2` is the OpenPGP part of the GNU Privacy Guard (GnuPG). It is a tool to provide digital encryption and signing services using the OpenPGP standard. `gpg2` features complete key management and all bells and whistles you can expect from a decent OpenPGP implementation.

In contrast to the standalone command gpg from GnuPG 1.x, which is might be better suited for server and embedded platforms, the 2.x version is commonly installed under the name `gpg2` and targeted to the desktop as it requires several other modules to be installed.

The old 1.x version will be kept maintained and it is possible to install both versions on the same system. Documentation for the old GnuPG 1.x command is available as a man page and at See Info file 'gpg', node 'Top'.

See [Option Index], page 167, for an index to `gpg2`'s commands and options.

4.1 Commands

Commands are not distinguished from options except for the fact that only one command is allowed.

`gpg2` may be run with no commands, in which case it will perform a reasonable action depending on the type of file it is given as input (an encrypted message is decrypted, a signature is verified, a file containing keys is listed).

Please remember that option as well as command parsing stops as soon as a non-option is encountered, you can explicitly stop parsing by using the special option '--'.

4.1.1 Commands not specific to the function

`--version`

> Print the program version and licensing information. Note that you cannot abbreviate this command.

`--help`
`-h`

> Print a usage message summarizing the most useful command line options. Note that you cannot abbreviate this command.

`--warranty`

> Print warranty information.

`--dump-options`

> Print a list of all available options and commands. Note that you cannot abbreviate this command.

4.1.2 Commands to select the type of operation

`--sign`
`-s`

> Make a signature. This command may be combined with '`--encrypt`' (for a signed and encrypted message), '`--symmetric`' (for a signed and symmetrically encrypted message), or '`--encrypt`' and '`--symmetric`' together (for a signed message that may be decrypted via a secret key or a passphrase). The key to be used for signing is chosen by default or can be set with the '`--local-user`' and '`--default-key`' options.

`--clearsign`
> Make a clear text signature. The content in a clear text signature is readable without any special software. OpenPGP software is only needed to verify the signature. Clear text signatures may modify end-of-line whitespace for platform independence and are not intended to be reversible. The key to be used for signing is chosen by default or can be set with the '`--local-user`' and '`--default-key`' options.

`--detach-sign`
`-b`
> Make a detached signature.

`--encrypt`
`-e`
> Encrypt data. This option may be combined with '`--sign`' (for a signed and encrypted message), '`--symmetric`' (for a message that may be decrypted via a secret key or a passphrase), or '`--sign`' and '`--symmetric`' together (for a signed message that may be decrypted via a secret key or a passphrase).

`--symmetric`
`-c`
> Encrypt with a symmetric cipher using a passphrase. The default symmetric cipher used is AES-128, but may be chosen with the '`--cipher-algo`' option. This option may be combined with '`--sign`' (for a signed and symmetrically encrypted message), '`--encrypt`' (for a message that may be decrypted via a secret key or a passphrase), or '`--sign`' and '`--encrypt`' together (for a signed message that may be decrypted via a secret key or a passphrase).

`--store`   Store only (make a simple RFC1991 literal data packet).

`--decrypt`
`-d`
> Decrypt the file given on the command line (or STDIN if no file is specified) and write it to STDOUT (or the file specified with '`--output`'). If the decrypted file is signed, the signature is also verified. This command differs from the default operation, as it never writes to the filename which is included in the file and it rejects files which don't begin with an encrypted message.

`--verify` Assume that the first argument is a signed file and verify it without generating any output. With no arguments, the signature packet is read from STDIN. If only a one argument is given, it is expected to be a complete signature.

> With more than 1 argument, the first should be a detached signature and the remaining files ake up the the signed data. To read the signed data from STDIN, use '`-`' as the second filename. For security reasons a detached signature cannot read the signed material from STDIN without denoting it in the above way.

> Note: If the option '`--batch`' is not used, **gpg2** may assume that a single argument is a file with a detached signature and it will try to find a matching data file by stripping certain suffixes. Using this historical feature to verify a detached signature is strongly discouraged; always specify the data file too.

> Note: When verifying a cleartext signature, **gpg** verifies only what makes up the cleartext signed data and not any extra data outside of the cleartext signature or header lines following directly the dash marker line. The option `--output` may be used to write out the actual signed data; but there are other pitfalls

with this format as well. It is suggested to avoid cleartext signatures in favor of detached signatures.

`--multifile`

> This modifies certain other commands to accept multiple files for processing on the command line or read from STDIN with each filename on a separate line. This allows for many files to be processed at once. '--multifile' may currently be used along with '--verify', '--encrypt', and '--decrypt'. Note that '--multifile --verify' may not be used with detached signatures.

`--verify-files`

> Identical to '--multifile --verify'.

`--encrypt-files`

> Identical to '--multifile --encrypt'.

`--decrypt-files`

> Identical to '--multifile --decrypt'.

`--list-keys`
`-k`
`--list-public-keys`

> List all keys from the public keyrings, or just the keys given on the command line.
>
> Avoid using the output of this command in scripts or other programs as it is likely to change as GnuPG changes. See '--with-colons' for a machine-parseable key listing command that is appropriate for use in scripts and other programs.

`--list-secret-keys`

`-K`   List all keys from the secret keyrings, or just the ones given on the command line. A # after the letters sec means that the secret key is not usable (for example, if it was created via '--export-secret-subkeys').

`--list-sigs`

> Same as '--list-keys', but the signatures are listed too. This command has the same effect as using '--list-keys' with '--with-sig-list'.
>
> For each signature listed, there are several flags in between the "sig" tag and keyid. These flags give additional information about each signature. From left to right, they are the numbers 1-3 for certificate check level (see '--ask-cert-level'), "L" for a local or non-exportable signature (see '--lsign-key'), "R" for a nonRevocable signature (see the '--edit-key' command "nrsign"), "P" for a signature that contains a policy URL (see '--cert-policy-url'), "N" for a signature that contains a notation (see '--cert-notation'), "X" for an eXpired signature (see '--ask-cert-expire'), and the numbers 1-9 or "T" for 10 and above to indicate trust signature levels (see the '--edit-key' command "tsign").

`--check-sigs`

> Same as '--list-sigs', but the signatures are verified. Note that for performance reasons the revocation status of a signing key is not shown. This command has the same effect as using '--list-keys' with '--with-sig-check'.

The status of the verification is indicated by a flag directly following the "sig" tag (and thus before the flags described above for '--list-sigs'). A "!" indicates that the signature has been successfully verified, a "-" denotes a bad signature and a "%" is used if an error occurred while checking the signature (e.g. a non supported algorithm).

--locate-keys

Locate the keys given as arguments. This command basically uses the same algorithm as used when locating keys for encryption or signing and may thus be used to see what keys gpg2 might use. In particular external methods as defined by '--auto-key-locate' may be used to locate a key. Only public keys are listed.

--fingerprint

List all keys (or the specified ones) along with their fingerprints. This is the same output as '--list-keys' but with the additional output of a line with the fingerprint. May also be combined with '--list-sigs' or '--check-sigs'. If this command is given twice, the fingerprints of all secondary keys are listed too.

--list-packets

List only the sequence of packets. This is mainly useful for debugging. When used with option '--verbose' the actual MPI values are dumped and not only their lengths.

--card-edit

Present a menu to work with a smartcard. The subcommand "help" provides an overview on available commands. For a detailed description, please see the Card HOWTO at https://gnupg.org/documentation/howtos.html#GnuPG-cardHOWTO .

--card-status

Show the content of the smart card.

--change-pin

Present a menu to allow changing the PIN of a smartcard. This functionality is also available as the subcommand "passwd" with the '--card-edit' command.

--delete-keys name
--delete-keys name

Remove key from the public keyring. In batch mode either '--yes' is required or the key must be specified by fingerprint. This is a safeguard against accidental deletion of multiple keys.

--delete-secret-keys name

Remove key from the secret keyring. In batch mode the key must be specified by fingerprint.

--delete-secret-and-public-key name

Same as '--delete-key', but if a secret key exists, it will be removed first. In batch mode the key must be specified by fingerprint.

--export   Either export all keys from all keyrings (default keyrings and those registered via option '--keyring'), or if at least one name is given, those of the given name. The exported keys are written to STDOUT or to the file given with option '--output'. Use together with '--armor' to mail those keys.

--send-keys key IDs

Similar to '--export' but sends the keys to a keyserver. Fingerprints may be used instead of key IDs. Option '--keyserver' must be used to give the name of this keyserver. Don't send your complete keyring to a keyserver — select only those keys which are new or changed by you. If no key IDs are given, gpg does nothing.

--export-secret-keys
--export-secret-subkeys

Same as '--export', but exports the secret keys instead. The exported keys are written to STDOUT or to the file given with option '--output'. This command is often used along with the option '--armor' to allow easy printing of the key for paper backup; however the external tool **paperkey** does a better job for creating backups on paper. Note that exporting a secret key can be a security risk if the exported keys are send over an insecure channel.

The second form of the command has the special property to render the secret part of the primary key useless; this is a GNU extension to OpenPGP and other implementations can not be expected to successfully import such a key. Its intended use is to generated a full key with an additional signing subkey on a dedicated machine and then using this command to export the key without the primary key to the main machine.

GnuPG may ask you to enter the passphrase for the key. This is required because the internal protection method of the secret key is different from the one specified by the OpenPGP protocol.

--import
--fast-import

Import/merge keys. This adds the given keys to the keyring. The fast version is currently just a synonym.

There are a few other options which control how this command works. Most notable here is the '--import-options merge-only' option which does not insert new keys but does only the merging of new signatures, user-IDs and subkeys.

--recv-keys key IDs

Import the keys with the given key IDs from a keyserver. Option '--keyserver' must be used to give the name of this keyserver.

--refresh-keys

Request updates from a keyserver for keys that already exist on the local keyring. This is useful for updating a key with the latest signatures, user IDs, etc. Calling this with no arguments will refresh the entire keyring. Option '--keyserver' must be used to give the name of the keyserver for all keys that do not have preferred keyservers set (see '--keyserver-options honor-keyserver-url').

`--search-keys names`

> Search the keyserver for the given names. Multiple names given here will be joined together to create the search string for the keyserver. Option '`--keyserver`' must be used to give the name of this keyserver. Keyservers that support different search methods allow using the syntax specified in "How to specify a user ID" below. Note that different keyserver types support different search methods. Currently only LDAP supports them all.

`--fetch-keys URIs`

> Retrieve keys located at the specified URIs. Note that different installations of GnuPG may support different protocols (HTTP, FTP, LDAP, etc.)

`--update-trustdb`

> Do trust database maintenance. This command iterates over all keys and builds the Web of Trust. This is an interactive command because it may have to ask for the "ownertrust" values for keys. The user has to give an estimation of how far she trusts the owner of the displayed key to correctly certify (sign) other keys. GnuPG only asks for the ownertrust value if it has not yet been assigned to a key. Using the '`--edit-key`' menu, the assigned value can be changed at any time.

`--check-trustdb`

> Do trust database maintenance without user interaction. From time to time the trust database must be updated so that expired keys or signatures and the resulting changes in the Web of Trust can be tracked. Normally, GnuPG will calculate when this is required and do it automatically unless '`--no-auto-check-trustdb`' is set. This command can be used to force a trust database check at any time. The processing is identical to that of '`--update-trustdb`' but it skips keys with a not yet defined "ownertrust".
>
> For use with cron jobs, this command can be used together with '`--batch`' in which case the trust database check is done only if a check is needed. To force a run even in batch mode add the option '`--yes`'.

`--export-ownertrust`

> Send the ownertrust values to STDOUT. This is useful for backup purposes as these values are the only ones which can't be re-created from a corrupted trustdb. Example:
>
> ```
> gpg2
> --export-ownertrust > otrust.txt
> ```

`--import-ownertrust`

> Update the trustdb with the ownertrust values stored in **files** (or STDIN if not given); existing values will be overwritten. In case of a severely damaged trustdb and if you have a recent backup of the ownertrust values (e.g. in the file '`otrust.txt`', you may re-create the trustdb using these commands:
>
> ```
> cd ~/.gnupg
> rm trustdb.gpg
> gpg2
> --import-ownertrust < otrust.txt
> ```

`--rebuild-keydb-caches`

>   When updating from version 1.0.6 to 1.0.7 this command should be used to create signature caches in the keyring. It might be handy in other situations too.

`--print-md algo`

`--print-mds`

>   Print message digest of algorithm ALGO for all given files or STDIN. With the second form (or a deprecated "*" as algo) digests for all available algorithms are printed.

`--gen-random 0|1|2 count`

>   Emit *count* random bytes of the given quality level 0, 1 or 2. If *count* is not given or zero, an endless sequence of random bytes will be emitted. If used with '`--armor`' the output will be base64 encoded. PLEASE, don't use this command unless you know what you are doing; it may remove precious entropy from the system!

`--gen-prime mode bits`

>   Use the source, Luke :-). The output format is still subject to change.

`--enarmor`

`--dearmor`

>   Pack or unpack an arbitrary input into/from an OpenPGP ASCII armor. This is a GnuPG extension to OpenPGP and in general not very useful.

4.1.3 How to manage your keys

This section explains the main commands for key management

`--quick-gen-key user-id`

>   This is a simple command to generate a standard key with one user id. In contrast to '`--gen-key`' the key is generated directly without the need to answer a bunch of prompts. Unless the option '`--yes`' is given, the key creation will be canceled if the given user id already exists in the key ring.
>
>   If invoked directly on the console without any special options an answer to a "Continue?" style confirmation prompt is required. In case the user id already exists in the key ring a second prompt to force the creation of the key will show up.
>
>   If this command is used with '`--batch`', '`--pinentry-mode`' has been set to `loopback`, and one of the passphrase options ('`--passphrase`', '`--passphrase-fd`', or '`passphrase-file`') is used, the supplied passphrase is used for the new key and the agent does not ask for it. To create a key without any protection `--passphrase` '' may be used.

`--gen-key`

>   Generate a new key pair using the current default parameters. This is the standard command to create a new key.

`--full-gen-key`

>   Generate a new key pair with dialogs for all options. This is an extended version of '`--gen-key`'.

There is also a feature which allows you to create keys in batch mode. See the
the manual section "Unattended key generation" on how to use this.

`--gen-revoke name`

> Generate a revocation certificate for the complete key. To revoke a subkey or a
> signature, use the '`--edit`' command.

`--desig-revoke name`

> Generate a designated revocation certificate for a key. This allows a user (with
> the permission of the keyholder) to revoke someone else's key.

`--edit-key`

> Present a menu which enables you to do most of the key management related
> tasks. It expects the specification of a key on the command line.

> | | |
> |---|---|
> | uid **n** | Toggle selection of user ID or photographic user ID with index **n**. Use * to select all and 0 to deselect all. |
> | key **n** | Toggle selection of subkey with index **n**. Use * to select all and 0 to deselect all. |
> | sign | Make a signature on key of user **name** If the key is not yet signed by the default user (or the users given with -u), the program displays the information of the key again, together with its fingerprint and asks whether it should be signed. This question is repeated for all users specified with -u. |
> | lsign | Same as "sign" but the signature is marked as non-exportable and will therefore never be used by others. This may be used to make keys valid only in the local environment. |
> | nrsign | Same as "sign" but the signature is marked as non-revocable and can therefore never be revoked. |
> | tsign | Make a trust signature. This is a signature that combines the notions of certification (like a regular signature), and trust (like the "trust" command). It is generally only useful in distinct communities or groups. |

> Note that "l" (for local / non-exportable), "nr" (for non-revocable, and "t"
> (for trust) may be freely mixed and prefixed to "sign" to create a signature of
> any type desired.

> | | |
> |---|---|
> | delsig | Delete a signature. Note that it is not possible to retract a signature, once it has been send to the public (i.e. to a keyserver). In that case you better use **revsig**. |
> | revsig | Revoke a signature. For every signature which has been generated by one of the secret keys, GnuPG asks whether a revocation certificate should be generated. |
> | check | Check the signatures on all selected user IDs. With the extra option **selfsig** only self-signatures are shown. |
> | adduid | Create an additional user ID. |

addphoto   Create a photographic user ID. This will prompt for a JPEG file
                 that will be embedded into the user ID. Note that a very large JPEG
                 will make for a very large key. Also note that some programs will
                 display your JPEG unchanged (GnuPG), and some programs will
                 scale it to fit in a dialog box (PGP).

showphoto
                 Display the selected photographic user ID.

deluid   Delete a user ID or photographic user ID. Note that it is not possible
                 to retract a user id, once it has been send to the public (i.e. to a
                 keyserver). In that case you better use **revuid**.

revuid   Revoke a user ID or photographic user ID.

primary   Flag the current user id as the primary one, removes the primary
                 user id flag from all other user ids and sets the timestamp of all
                 affected self-signatures one second ahead. Note that setting a photo
                 user ID as primary makes it primary over other photo user IDs, and
                 setting a regular user ID as primary makes it primary over other
                 regular user IDs.

keyserver   Set a preferred keyserver for the specified user ID(s). This allows
                 other users to know where you prefer they get your key from. See
                 '**--keyserver-options honor-keyserver-url**' for more on how
                 this works. Setting a value of "none" removes an existing preferred
                 keyserver.

notation   Set a name=value notation for the specified user ID(s). See
                 '**--cert-notation**' for more on how this works. Setting a value
                 of "none" removes all notations, setting a notation prefixed with
                 a minus sign (-) removes that notation, and setting a notation
                 name (without the =value) prefixed with a minus sign removes all
                 notations with that name.

pref   List preferences from the selected user ID. This shows the actual
                 preferences, without including any implied preferences.

showpref   More verbose preferences listing for the selected user ID. This shows
                 the preferences in effect by including the implied preferences of
                 3DES (cipher), SHA-1 (digest), and Uncompressed (compression)
                 if they are not already included in the preference list. In addition,
                 the preferred keyserver and signature notations (if any) are shown.

setpref **string**
                 Set the list of user ID preferences to **string** for all (or just
                 the selected) user IDs. Calling setpref with no arguments sets
                 the preference list to the default (either built-in or set via
                 '**--default-preference-list**'), and calling setpref with "none"
                 as the argument sets an empty preference list. Use **gpg2--version**
                 to get a list of available algorithms. Note that while you can
                 change the preferences on an attribute user ID (aka "photo ID"),

GnuPG does not select keys via attribute user IDs so these preferences will not be used by GnuPG.

When setting preferences, you should list the algorithms in the order which you'd like to see them used by someone else when encrypting a message to your key. If you don't include 3DES, it will be automatically added at the end. Note that there are many factors that go into choosing an algorithm (for example, your key may not be the only recipient), and so the remote OpenPGP application being used to send to you may or may not follow your exact chosen order for a given message. It will, however, only choose an algorithm that is present on the preference list of every recipient key. See also the INTEROPERABILITY WITH OTHER OPENPGP PROGRAMS section below.

addkey   Add a subkey to this key.

addcardkey
            Generate a subkey on a card and add it to this key.

keytocard   Transfer the selected secret subkey (or the primary key if no subkey has been selected) to a smartcard. The secret key in the keyring will be replaced by a stub if the key could be stored successfully on the card and you use the save command later. Only certain key types may be transferred to the card. A sub menu allows you to select on what card to store the key. Note that it is not possible to get that key back from the card - if the card gets broken your secret key will be lost unless you have a backup somewhere.

bkuptocard `file`
            Restore the given file to a card. This command may be used to restore a backup key (as generated during card initialization) to a new card. In almost all cases this will be the encryption key. You should use this command only with the corresponding public key and make sure that the file given as argument is indeed the backup to restore. You should then select 2 to restore as encryption key. You will first be asked to enter the passphrase of the backup key and then for the Admin PIN of the card.

delkey   Remove a subkey (secondary key). Note that it is not possible to retract a subkey, once it has been send to the public (i.e. to a keyserver). In that case you better use `revkey`.

revkey   Revoke a subkey.

expire   Change the key or subkey expiration time. If a subkey is selected, the expiration time of this subkey will be changed. With no selection, the key expiration of the primary key is changed.

trust   Change the owner trust value for the key. This updates the trust-db immediately and no save is required.

disable

enable   Disable or enable an entire key. A disabled key can not normally
                 be used for encryption.

addrevoker

                 Add a designated revoker to the key. This takes one optional argu-
                 ment: "sensitive". If a designated revoker is marked as sensitive,
                 it will not be exported by default (see export-options).

passwd   Change the passphrase of the secret key.

toggle   This is dummy command which exists only for backward compati-
                 bility.

clean   Compact (by removing all signatures except the selfsig) any user
                 ID that is no longer usable (e.g. revoked, or expired). Then, re-
                 move any signatures that are not usable by the trust calculations.
                 Specifically, this removes any signature that does not validate, any
                 signature that is superseded by a later signature, revoked signa-
                 tures, and signatures issued by keys that are not present on the
                 keyring.

minimize   Make the key as small as possible. This removes all signatures from
                 each user ID except for the most recent self-signature.

cross-certify

                 Add cross-certification signatures to signing subkeys that
                 may not currently have them. Cross-certification signatures
                 protect against a subtle attack against signing subkeys. See
                 '--require-cross-certification'. All new keys generated have
                 this signature by default, so this option is only useful to bring
                 older keys up to date.

save   Save all changes to the key rings and quit.

quit   Quit the program without updating the key rings.

The listing shows you the key with its secondary keys and all user ids. The
primary user id is indicated by a dot, and selected keys or user ids are indicated
by an asterisk. The trust value is displayed with the primary key: the first is
the assigned owner trust and the second is the calculated trust value. Letters
are used for the values:

-                No ownertrust assigned / not yet calculated.

e   Trust calculation has failed; probably due to an expired key.

q   Not enough information for calculation.

n   Never trust this key.

m   Marginally trusted.

f   Fully trusted.

u   Ultimately trusted.

`--sign-key name`

> Signs a public key with your secret key. This is a shortcut version of the subcommand "sign" from '`--edit`'.

`--lsign-key name`

> Signs a public key with your secret key but marks it as non-exportable. This is a shortcut version of the subcommand "lsign" from '`--edit-key`'.

`--quick-sign-key fpr [names]`
`--quick-lsign-key fpr [names]`

> Directly sign a key from the passphrase without any further user interaction. The `fpr` must be the verified primary fingerprint of a key in the local keyring. If no `names` are given, all useful user ids are signed; with given [`names`] only useful user ids matching one of theses names are signed. The command '`--quick-lsign-key`' marks the signatures as non-exportable. If such a non-exportable signature already exists the '`--quick-sign-key`' turns it into a exportable signature.
>
> This command uses reasonable defaults and thus does not provide the full flexibility of the "sign" subcommand from '`--edit-key`'. Its intended use is to help unattended key signing by utilizing a list of verified fingerprints.

`--quick-adduid user-id new-user-id`

> This command adds a new user id to an existing key. In contrast to the interactive sub-command `adduid` of '`--edit-key`' the *new-user-id* is added verbatim with only leading and trailing white space removed, it is expected to be UTF-8 encoded, and no checks on its form are applied.

`--passwd user_id`

> Change the passphrase of the secret key belonging to the certificate specified as *user_id*. This is a shortcut for the sub-command `passwd` of the edit key menu.

4.2 Option Summary

`gpg2` features a bunch of options to control the exact behaviour and to change the default configuration.

Long options can be put in an options file (default `"~/.gnupg/gpg.conf"`). Short option names will not work - for example, "armor" is a valid option for the options file, while "a" is not. Do not write the 2 dashes, but simply the name of the option and any required arguments. Lines with a hash ('#') as the first non-white-space character are ignored. Commands may be put in this file too, but that is not generally useful as the command will execute automatically with every execution of gpg.

Please remember that option parsing stops as soon as a non-option is encountered, you can explicitly stop parsing by using the special option '`--`'.

4.2.1 How to change the configuration

These options are used to change the configuration and are usually found in the option file.

`--default-key` *name*

> Use *name* as the default key to sign with. If this option is not used, the default key is the first key found in the secret keyring. Note that '`-u`' or '`--local-user`' overrides this option.

`--default-recipient` *name*

> Use *name* as default recipient if option '`--recipient`' is not used and don't ask if this is a valid one. *name* must be non-empty.

`--default-recipient-self`

> Use the default key as default recipient if option '`--recipient`' is not used and don't ask if this is a valid one. The default key is the first one from the secret keyring or the one set with '`--default-key`'.

`--no-default-recipient`

> Reset '`--default-recipient`' and '`--default-recipient-self`'.

`-v, --verbose`

> Give more information during processing. If used twice, the input data is listed in detail.

`--no-verbose`

> Reset verbose level to 0.

`-q, --quiet`

> Try to be as quiet as possible.

`--batch`
`--no-batch`

> Use batch mode. Never ask, do not allow interactive commands. '`--no-batch`' disables this option. Note that even with a filename given on the command line, gpg might still need to read from STDIN (in particular if gpg figures that the input is a detached signature and no data file has been specified). Thus if you do not want to feed data via STDIN, you should connect STDIN to '`/dev/null`'.

`--no-tty` Make sure that the TTY (terminal) is never used for any output. This option is needed in some cases because GnuPG sometimes prints warnings to the TTY even if '`--batch`' is used.

`--yes`   Assume "yes" on most questions.

`--no`   Assume "no" on most questions.

`--list-options` *parameters*

> This is a space or comma delimited string that gives options used when listing keys and signatures (that is, '`--list-keys`', '`--list-sigs`', '`--list-public-keys`', '`--list-secret-keys`', and the '`--edit-key`' functions). Options can be prepended with a '`no-`' (after the two dashes) to give the opposite meaning. The options are:
>
> show-photos
>
> > Causes '`--list-keys`', '`--list-sigs`', '`--list-public-keys`', and '`--list-secret-keys`' to display any photo IDs attached

to the key. Defaults to no. See also '--photo-viewer'. Does
not work with '--with-colons': see '--attribute-fd' for the
appropriate way to get photo data for scripts and other frontends.

show-usage

Show usage information for keys and subkeys in the standard key
listing. This is a list of letters indicating the allowed usage for a
key (E=encryption, S=signing, C=certification, A=authentication).
Defaults to no.

show-policy-urls

Show policy URLs in the '--list-sigs' or '--check-sigs' listings.
Defaults to no.

show-notations
show-std-notations
show-user-notations

Show all, IETF standard, or user-defined signature notations in the
'--list-sigs' or '--check-sigs' listings. Defaults to no.

show-keyserver-urls

Show any preferred keyserver URL in the '--list-sigs' or
'--check-sigs' listings. Defaults to no.

show-uid-validity

Display the calculated validity of user IDs during key listings. Defaults to no.

show-unusable-uids

Show revoked and expired user IDs in key listings. Defaults to no.

show-unusable-subkeys

Show revoked and expired subkeys in key listings. Defaults to no.

show-keyring

Display the keyring name at the head of key listings to show which
keyring a given key resides on. Defaults to no.

show-sig-expire

Show signature expiration dates (if any) during '--list-sigs' or
'--check-sigs' listings. Defaults to no.

show-sig-subpackets

Include signature subpackets in the key listing. This option can take
an optional argument list of the subpackets to list. If no argument
is passed, list all subpackets. Defaults to no. This option is only
meaningful when using '--with-colons' along with '--list-sigs'
or '--check-sigs'.

--verify-options parameters

This is a space or comma delimited string that gives options used when verifying
signatures. Options can be prepended with a 'no-' to give the opposite meaning.
The options are:

show-photos

> Display any photo IDs present on the key that issued the signature. Defaults to no. See also '--photo-viewer'.

show-policy-urls

> Show policy URLs in the signature being verified. Defaults to no.

show-notations
show-std-notations
show-user-notations

> Show all, IETF standard, or user-defined signature notations in the signature being verified. Defaults to IETF standard.

show-keyserver-urls

> Show any preferred keyserver URL in the signature being verified. Defaults to no.

show-uid-validity

> Display the calculated validity of the user IDs on the key that issued the signature. Defaults to no.

show-unusable-uids

> Show revoked and expired user IDs during signature verification. Defaults to no.

show-primary-uid-only

> Show only the primary user ID during signature verification. That is all the AKA lines as well as photo Ids are not shown with the signature verification status.

pka-lookups

> Enable PKA lookups to verify sender addresses. Note that PKA is based on DNS, and so enabling this option may disclose information on when and what signatures are verified or to whom data is encrypted. This is similar to the "web bug" described for the auto-key-retrieve feature.

pka-trust-increase

> Raise the trust in a signature to full if the signature passes PKA validation. This option is only meaningful if pka-lookups is set.

--enable-large-rsa
--disable-large-rsa

> With –gen-key and –batch, enable the creation of larger RSA secret keys than is generally recommended (up to 8192 bits). These large keys are more expensive to use, and their signatures and certifications are also larger.

--enable-dsa2
--disable-dsa2

> Enable hash truncation for all DSA keys even for old DSA Keys up to 1024 bit. This is also the default with '--openpgp'. Note that older versions of GnuPG also required this flag to allow the generation of DSA larger than 1024 bit.

--photo-viewer string

> This is the command line that should be run to view a photo ID. "%i" will be expanded to a filename containing the photo. "%I" does the same, except the file will not be deleted once the viewer exits. Other flags are "%k" for the key ID, "%K" for the long key ID, "%f" for the key fingerprint, "%t" for the extension of the image type (e.g. "jpg"), "%T" for the MIME type of the image (e.g. "image/jpeg"), "%v" for the single-character calculated validity of the image being viewed (e.g. "f"), "%V" for the calculated validity as a string (e.g. "full"), "%U" for a base32 encoded hash of the user ID, and "%%" for an actual percent sign. If neither %i or %I are present, then the photo will be supplied to the viewer on standard input.
>
> The default viewer is "xloadimage -fork -quiet -title 'KeyID 0x%k' STDIN". Note that if your image viewer program is not secure, then executing it from GnuPG does not make it secure.

--exec-path string

> Sets a list of directories to search for photo viewers and keyserver helpers. If not provided, keyserver helpers use the compiled-in default directory, and photo viewers use the $PATH environment variable. Note, that on W32 system this value is ignored when searching for keyserver helpers.

--keyring file

> Add `file` to the current list of keyrings. If `file` begins with a tilde and a slash, these are replaced by the $HOME directory. If the filename does not contain a slash, it is assumed to be in the GnuPG home directory ("~/.gnupg" if '--homedir' or $GNUPGHOME is not used).
>
> Note that this adds a keyring to the current list. If the intent is to use the specified keyring alone, use '--keyring' along with '--no-default-keyring'.

--secret-keyring file

> This is an obsolete option and ignored. All secret keys are stored in the 'private-keys-v1.d' directory below the GnuPG home directory.

--primary-keyring file

> Designate `file` as the primary public keyring. This means that newly imported keys (via '--import' or keyserver '--recv-from') will go to this keyring.

--trustdb-name file

> Use `file` instead of the default trustdb. If `file` begins with a tilde and a slash, these are replaced by the $HOME directory. If the filename does not contain a slash, it is assumed to be in the GnuPG home directory ('~/.gnupg' if '--homedir' or $GNUPGHOME is not used).

--homedir dir

> Set the name of the home directory to *dir*. If this option is not used, the home directory defaults to '~/.gnupg'. It is only recognized when given on the command line. It also overrides any home directory stated through the environment variable GNUPGHOME or (on Windows systems) by means of the Registry entry *HKCU\Software\GNU\GnuPG:HomeDir*.

On Windows systems it is possible to install GnuPG as a portable application. In this case only this command line option is considered, all other ways to set a home directory are ignored.

To install GnuPG as a portable application under Windows, create an empty file name 'gpgconf.ctl' in the same directory as the tool 'gpgconf.exe'. The root of the installation is than that directory; or, if 'gpgconf.exe' has been installed directly below a directory named 'bin', its parent directory. You also need to make sure that the following directories exist and are writable: 'ROOT/home' for the GnuPG home and 'ROOT/usr/local/var/cache/gnupg' for internal cache files.

`--display-charset name`

Set the name of the native character set. This is used to convert some informational strings like user IDs to the proper UTF-8 encoding. Note that this has nothing to do with the character set of data to be encrypted or signed; GnuPG does not recode user-supplied data. If this option is not used, the default character set is determined from the current locale. A verbosity level of 3 shows the chosen set. Valid values for `name` are:

iso-8859-1   This is the Latin 1 set.

iso-8859-2   The Latin 2 set.

iso-8859-15
             This is currently an alias for the Latin 1 set.

koi8-r   The usual Russian set (rfc1489).

utf-8   Bypass all translations and assume that the OS uses native UTF-8 encoding.

`--utf8-strings`
`--no-utf8-strings`

Assume that command line arguments are given as UTF8 strings. The default ('`--no-utf8-strings`') is to assume that arguments are encoded in the character set as specified by '`--display-charset`'. These options affect all following arguments. Both options may be used multiple times.

`--options file`

Read options from `file` and do not try to read them from the default options file in the homedir (see '`--homedir`'). This option is ignored if used in an options file.

`--no-options`

Shortcut for '`--options /dev/null`'. This option is detected before an attempt to open an option file. Using this option will also prevent the creation of a '`~/.gnupg`' homedir.

`-z n`
`--compress-level n`
`--bzip2-compress-level n`

Set compression level to `n` for the ZIP and ZLIB compression algorithms. The default is to use the default compression level of zlib (normally 6).

'--bzip2-compress-level' sets the compression level for the BZIP2 compression algorithm (defaulting to 6 as well). This is a different option from '--compress-level' since BZIP2 uses a significant amount of memory for each additional compression level. '-z' sets both. A value of 0 for n disables compression.

--bzip2-decompress-lowmem

Use a different decompression method for BZIP2 compressed files. This alternate method uses a bit more than half the memory, but also runs at half the speed. This is useful under extreme low memory circumstances when the file was originally compressed at a high '--bzip2-compress-level'.

--mangle-dos-filenames
--no-mangle-dos-filenames

Older version of Windows cannot handle filenames with more than one dot. '--mangle-dos-filenames' causes GnuPG to replace (rather than add to) the extension of an output filename to avoid this problem. This option is off by default and has no effect on non-Windows platforms.

--ask-cert-level
--no-ask-cert-level

When making a key signature, prompt for a certification level. If this option is not specified, the certification level used is set via '--default-cert-level'. See '--default-cert-level' for information on the specific levels and how they are used. '--no-ask-cert-level' disables this option. This option defaults to no.

--default-cert-level n

The default to use for the check level when signing a key.

0 means you make no particular claim as to how carefully you verified the key.

1 means you believe the key is owned by the person who claims to own it but you could not, or did not verify the key at all. This is useful for a "persona" verification, where you sign the key of a pseudonymous user.

2 means you did casual verification of the key. For example, this could mean that you verified the key fingerprint and checked the user ID on the key against a photo ID.

3 means you did extensive verification of the key. For example, this could mean that you verified the key fingerprint with the owner of the key in person, and that you checked, by means of a hard to forge document with a photo ID (such as a passport) that the name of the key owner matches the name in the user ID on the key, and finally that you verified (by exchange of email) that the email address on the key belongs to the key owner.

Note that the examples given above for levels 2 and 3 are just that: examples. In the end, it is up to you to decide just what "casual" and "extensive" mean to you.

This option defaults to 0 (no particular claim).

`--min-cert-level`

> When building the trust database, treat any signatures with a certification level below this as invalid. Defaults to 2, which disregards level 1 signatures. Note that level 0 "no particular claim" signatures are always accepted.

`--trusted-key long key ID`

> Assume that the specified key (which must be given as a full 8 byte key ID) is as trustworthy as one of your own secret keys. This option is useful if you don't want to keep your secret keys (or one of them) online but still want to be able to check the validity of a given recipient's or signator's key.

`--trust-model pgp|classic|direct|always|auto`

> Set what trust model GnuPG should follow. The models are:

> pgp
> > This is the Web of Trust combined with trust signatures as used in PGP 5.x and later. This is the default trust model when creating a new trust database.

> classic
> > This is the standard Web of Trust as introduced by PGP 2.

> direct
> > Key validity is set directly by the user and not calculated via the Web of Trust.

> always
> > Skip key validation and assume that used keys are always fully valid. You generally won't use this unless you are using some external validation scheme. This option also suppresses the "[uncertain]" tag printed with signature checks when there is no evidence that the user ID is bound to the key. Note that this trust model still does not allow the use of expired, revoked, or disabled keys.

> auto
> > Select the trust model depending on whatever the internal trust database says. This is the default model if such a database already exists.

`--auto-key-locate parameters`
`--no-auto-key-locate`

> GnuPG can automatically locate and retrieve keys as needed using this option. This happens when encrypting to an email address (in the "user@example.com" form), and there are no user@example.com keys on the local keyring. This option takes any number of the following mechanisms, in the order they are to be tried:

> cert
> > Locate a key using DNS CERT, as specified in rfc4398.

> pka
> > Locate a key using DNS PKA.

> dane
> > Locate a key using DANE, as specified in draft-ietf-dane-openpgpkey-05.txt.

> ldap
> > Using DNS Service Discovery, check the domain in question for any LDAP keyservers to use. If this fails, attempt to locate the key using the PGP Universal method of checking `ldap://keys.(thedomain)`.

> keyserver
> > Locate a key using whatever keyserver is defined using the `--keyserver` option.

keyserver-URL

> In addition, a keyserver URL as used in the '--keyserver' option may be used here to query that particular keyserver.

local

> Locate the key using the local keyrings. This mechanism allows to select the order a local key lookup is done. Thus using '--auto-key-locate local' is identical to '--no-auto-key-locate'.

nodefault

> This flag disables the standard local key lookup, done before any of the mechanisms defined by the '--auto-key-locate' are tried. The position of this mechanism in the list does not matter. It is not required if local is also used.

clear

> Clear all defined mechanisms. This is useful to override mechanisms given in a config file.

--keyid-format short|0xshort|long|0xlong

> Select how to display key IDs. "short" is the traditional 8-character key ID. "long" is the more accurate (but less convenient) 16-character key ID. Add an "0x" to either to include an "0x" at the beginning of the key ID, as in 0x99242560. Note that this option is ignored if the option –with-colons is used.

--keyserver name

> This option is deprecated - please use the '--keyserver' in 'dirmngr.conf' instead.
>
> Use **name** as your keyserver. This is the server that '--recv-keys', '--send-keys', and '--search-keys' will communicate with to receive keys from, send keys to, and search for keys on. The format of the **name** is a URI: 'scheme:[//]keyservername[:port]' The scheme is the type of keyserver: "hkp" for the HTTP (or compatible) keyservers, "ldap" for the LDAP keyservers, or "mailto" for the Graff email keyserver. Note that your particular installation of GnuPG may have other keyserver types available as well. Keyserver schemes are case-insensitive. After the keyserver name, optional keyserver configuration options may be provided. These are the same as the global '--keyserver-options' from below, but apply only to this particular keyserver.
>
> Most keyservers synchronize with each other, so there is generally no need to send keys to more than one server. The keyserver hkp://keys.gnupg.net uses round robin DNS to give a different keyserver each time you use it.

--keyserver-options name=value

> This is a space or comma delimited string that gives options for the keyserver. Options can be prefixed with a 'no-' to give the opposite meaning. Valid import-options or export-options may be used here as well to apply to importing ('--recv-key') or exporting ('--send-key') a key from a keyserver. While not all options are available for all keyserver types, some common options are:
>
> include-revoked
>
> > When searching for a key with '--search-keys', include keys that are marked on the keyserver as revoked. Note that not all key-

servers differentiate between revoked and unrevoked keys, and for such keyservers this option is meaningless. Note also that most keyservers do not have cryptographic verification of key revocations, and so turning this option off may result in skipping keys that are incorrectly marked as revoked.

include-disabled

When searching for a key with '`--search-keys`', include keys that are marked on the keyserver as disabled. Note that this option is not used with HKP keyservers.

auto-key-retrieve

This option enables the automatic retrieving of keys from a keyserver when verifying signatures made by keys that are not on the local keyring.

Note that this option makes a "web bug" like behavior possible. Keyserver operators can see which keys you request, so by sending you a message signed by a brand new key (which you naturally will not have on your local keyring), the operator can tell both your IP address and the time when you verified the signature.

honor-keyserver-url

When using '`--refresh-keys`', if the key in question has a preferred keyserver URL, then use that preferred keyserver to refresh the key from. In addition, if auto-key-retrieve is set, and the signature being verified has a preferred keyserver URL, then use that preferred keyserver to fetch the key from. Note that this option introduces a "web bug": The creator of the key can see when the keys is refreshed. Thus this option is not enabled by default.

honor-pka-record

If auto-key-retrieve is set, and the signature being verified has a PKA record, then use the PKA information to fetch the key. Defaults to "yes".

include-subkeys

When receiving a key, include subkeys as potential targets. Note that this option is not used with HKP keyservers, as they do not support retrieving keys by subkey id.

timeout   Tell the keyserver helper program how long (in seconds) to try and perform a keyserver action before giving up. Note that performing multiple actions at the same time uses this timeout value per action. For example, when retrieving multiple keys via '`--recv-keys`', the timeout applies separately to each key retrieval, and not to the '`--recv-keys`' command as a whole. Defaults to 30 seconds.

http-proxy=`value`

This options is deprecated. Set the proxy to use for HTTP and HKP keyservers. This overrides any proxy defined in '`dirmngr.conf`'.

verbose   This option has no more function since GnuPG 2.1. Use the
               `dirmngr` configuration options instead.

debug   This option has no more function since GnuPG 2.1. Use the
               `dirmngr` configuration options instead.

check-cert   This option has no more function since GnuPG 2.1. Use the
               `dirmngr` configuration options instead.

ca-cert-file   This option has no more function since GnuPG 2.1. Use the
               `dirmngr` configuration options instead.

`--completes-needed n`
: Number of completely trusted users to introduce a new key signer (defaults to 1).

`--marginals-needed n`
: Number of marginally trusted users to introduce a new key signer (defaults to 3)

`--max-cert-depth n`
: Maximum depth of a certification chain (default is 5).

`--no-sig-cache`
: Do not cache the verification status of key signatures. Caching gives a much better performance in key listings. However, if you suspect that your public keyring is not save against write modifications, you can use this option to disable the caching. It probably does not make sense to disable it because all kind of damage can be done if someone else has write access to your public keyring.

`--auto-check-trustdb`
`--no-auto-check-trustdb`
: If GnuPG feels that its information about the Web of Trust has to be updated, it automatically runs the '`--check-trustdb`' command internally. This may be a time consuming process. '`--no-auto-check-trustdb`' disables this option.

`--use-agent`
`--no-use-agent`
: This is dummy option. `gpg2` always requires the agent.

`--gpg-agent-info`
: This is dummy option. It has no effect when used with `gpg2`.

`--agent-program file`
: Specify an agent program to be used for secret key operations. The default value is determined by running `gpgconf` with the option '`--list-dirs`'. Note that the pipe symbol (|) is used for a regression test suite hack and may thus not be used in the file name.

`--dirmngr-program file`
: Specify a dirmngr program to be used for keyserver access. The default value is '`/usr/local/bin/dirmngr`'. This is only used as a fallback when the environment variable `DIRMNGR_INFO` is not set or a running dirmngr cannot be connected.

`--no-autostart`

> Do not start the gpg-agent or the dirmngr if it has not yet been started and its service is required. This option is mostly useful on machines where the connection to gpg-agent has been redirected to another machines. If dirmngr is required on the remote machine, it may be started manually using `gpgconf --launch dirmngr`.

`--lock-once`

> Lock the databases the first time a lock is requested and do not release the lock until the process terminates.

`--lock-multiple`

> Release the locks every time a lock is no longer needed. Use this to override a previous '`--lock-once`' from a config file.

`--lock-never`

> Disable locking entirely. This option should be used only in very special environments, where it can be assured that only one process is accessing those files. A bootable floppy with a stand-alone encryption system will probably use this. Improper usage of this option may lead to data and key corruption.

`--exit-on-status-write-error`

> This option will cause write errors on the status FD to immediately terminate the process. That should in fact be the default but it never worked this way and thus we need an option to enable this, so that the change won't break applications which close their end of a status fd connected pipe too early. Using this option along with '`--enable-progress-filter`' may be used to cleanly cancel long running gpg operations.

`--limit-card-insert-tries n`

> With n greater than 0 the number of prompts asking to insert a smartcard gets limited to N-1. Thus with a value of 1 gpg won't at all ask to insert a card if none has been inserted at startup. This option is useful in the configuration file in case an application does not know about the smartcard support and waits ad infinitum for an inserted card.

`--no-random-seed-file`

> GnuPG uses a file to store its internal random pool over invocations. This makes random generation faster; however sometimes write operations are not desired. This option can be used to achieve that with the cost of slower random generation.

`--no-greeting`

> Suppress the initial copyright message.

`--no-secmem-warning`

> Suppress the warning about "using insecure memory".

`--no-permission-warning`

> Suppress the warning about unsafe file and home directory ('`--homedir`') permissions. Note that the permission checks that GnuPG performs are not intended to be authoritative, but rather they simply warn about certain common

permission problems. Do not assume that the lack of a warning means that your system is secure.

Note that the warning for unsafe '--homedir' permissions cannot be suppressed in the gpg.conf file, as this would allow an attacker to place an unsafe gpg.conf file in place, and use this file to suppress warnings about itself. The '--homedir' permissions warning may only be suppressed on the command line.

`--no-mdc-warning`

Suppress the warning about missing MDC integrity protection.

`--require-secmem`
`--no-require-secmem`

Refuse to run if GnuPG cannot get secure memory. Defaults to no (i.e. run, but give a warning).

`--require-cross-certification`
`--no-require-cross-certification`

When verifying a signature made from a subkey, ensure that the cross certification "back signature" on the subkey is present and valid. This protects against a subtle attack against subkeys that can sign. Defaults to '--require-cross-certification' for gpg2.

`--expert`
`--no-expert`

Allow the user to do certain nonsensical or "silly" things like signing an expired or revoked key, or certain potentially incompatible things like generating unusual key types. This also disables certain warning messages about potentially incompatible actions. As the name implies, this option is for experts only. If you don't fully understand the implications of what it allows you to do, leave this off. '--no-expert' disables this option.

4.2.2 Key related options

`--recipient name`
`-r`   Encrypt for user id name. If this option or '--hidden-recipient' is not specified, GnuPG asks for the user-id unless '--default-recipient' is given.

`--hidden-recipient name`
`-R`   Encrypt for user ID name, but hide the key ID of this user's key. This option helps to hide the receiver of the message and is a limited countermeasure against traffic analysis. If this option or '--recipient' is not specified, GnuPG asks for the user ID unless '--default-recipient' is given.

`--encrypt-to name`

Same as '--recipient' but this one is intended for use in the options file and may be used with your own user-id as an "encrypt-to-self". These keys are only used when there are other recipients given either by use of '--recipient' or by the asked user id. No trust checking is performed for these user ids and even disabled keys can be used.

`--hidden-encrypt-to name`

Same as '`--hidden-recipient`' but this one is intended for use in the options file and may be used with your own user-id as a hidden "encrypt-to-self". These keys are only used when there are other recipients given either by use of '`--recipient`' or by the asked user id. No trust checking is performed for these user ids and even disabled keys can be used.

`--no-encrypt-to`

Disable the use of all '`--encrypt-to`' and '`--hidden-encrypt-to`' keys.

`--group name=value1`

Sets up a named group, which is similar to aliases in email programs. Any time the group name is a recipient ('`-r`' or '`--recipient`'), it will be expanded to the values specified. Multiple groups with the same name are automatically merged into a single group.

The values are key IDs or fingerprints, but any key description is accepted. Note that a value with spaces in it will be treated as two different values. Note also there is only one level of expansion — you cannot make an group that points to another group. When used from the command line, it may be necessary to quote the argument to this option to prevent the shell from treating it as multiple arguments.

`--ungroup name`

Remove a given entry from the '`--group`' list.

`--no-groups`

Remove all entries from the '`--group`' list.

`--local-user name`

`-u`   Use *name* as the key to sign with. Note that this option overrides '`--default-key`'.

`--try-secret-key name`

For hidden recipients GPG needs to know the keys to use for trial decryption. The key set with '`--default-key`' is always tried first, but this is often not sufficient. This option allows to set more keys to be used for trial decryption. Although any valid user-id specification may be used for *name* it makes sense to use at least the long keyid to avoid ambiguities. Note that gpg-agent might pop up a pinentry for a lot keys to do the trial decryption. If you want to stop all further trial decryption you may use close-window button instead of the cancel button.

`--try-all-secrets`

Don't look at the key ID as stored in the message but try all secret keys in turn to find the right decryption key. This option forces the behaviour as used by anonymous recipients (created by using '`--throw-keyids`' or '`--hidden-recipient`') and might come handy in case where an encrypted message contains a bogus key ID.

`--skip-hidden-recipients`
`--no-skip-hidden-recipients`

> During decryption skip all anonymous recipients. This option helps in the case that people use the hidden recipients feature to hide there own encrypt-to key from others. If oneself has many secret keys this may lead to a major annoyance because all keys are tried in turn to decrypt something which was not really intended for it. The drawback of this option is that it is currently not possible to decrypt a message which includes real anonymous recipients.

4.2.3 Input and Output

`--armor`
`-a`   Create ASCII armored output. The default is to create the binary OpenPGP format.

`--no-armor`

> Assume the input data is not in ASCII armored format.

`--output` *file*
`-o` *file*   Write output to *file*.

`--max-output n`

> This option sets a limit on the number of bytes that will be generated when processing a file. Since OpenPGP supports various levels of compression, it is possible that the plaintext of a given message may be significantly larger than the original OpenPGP message. While GnuPG works properly with such messages, there is often a desire to set a maximum file size that will be generated before processing is forced to stop by the OS limits. Defaults to 0, which means "no limit".

`--import-options parameters`

> This is a space or comma delimited string that gives options for importing keys. Options can be prepended with a 'no-' to give the opposite meaning. The options are:
>
> import-local-sigs
>
> > Allow importing key signatures marked as "local". This is not generally useful unless a shared keyring scheme is being used. Defaults to no.
>
> keep-ownertrust
>
> > Normally possible still existing ownertrust values of a key are cleared if a key is imported. This is in general desirable so that a formerly deleted key does not automatically gain an ownertrust values merely due to import. On the other hand it is sometimes necessary to re-import a trusted set of keys again but keeping already assigned ownertrust values. This can be achived by using this option.
>
> repair-pks-subkey-bug
>
> > During import, attempt to repair the damage caused by the PKS keyserver bug (pre version 0.9.6) that mangles keys with multiple

subkeys. Note that this cannot completely repair the damaged key as some crucial data is removed by the keyserver, but it does at least give you back one subkey. Defaults to no for regular '--import' and to yes for keyserver '--recv-keys'.

merge-only

During import, allow key updates to existing keys, but do not allow any new keys to be imported. Defaults to no.

import-clean

After import, compact (remove all signatures except the self-signature) any user IDs from the new key that are not usable. Then, remove any signatures from the new key that are not usable. This includes signatures that were issued by keys that are not present on the keyring. This option is the same as running the '--edit-key' command "clean" after import. Defaults to no.

import-minimal

Import the smallest key possible. This removes all signatures except the most recent self-signature on each user ID. This option is the same as running the '--edit-key' command "minimize" after import. Defaults to no.

--export-options parameters

This is a space or comma delimited string that gives options for exporting keys. Options can be prepended with a 'no-' to give the opposite meaning. The options are:

export-local-sigs

Allow exporting key signatures marked as "local". This is not generally useful unless a shared keyring scheme is being used. Defaults to no.

export-attributes

Include attribute user IDs (photo IDs) while exporting. This is useful to export keys if they are going to be used by an OpenPGP program that does not accept attribute user IDs. Defaults to yes.

export-sensitive-revkeys

Include designated revoker information that was marked as "sensitive". Defaults to no.

export-clean

Compact (remove all signatures from) user IDs on the key being exported if the user IDs are not usable. Also, do not export any signatures that are not usable. This includes signatures that were issued by keys that are not present on the keyring. This option is the same as running the '--edit-key' command "clean" before export except that the local copy of the key is not modified. Defaults to no.

export-minimal

> Export the smallest key possible. This removes all signatures except the most recent self-signature on each user ID. This option is the same as running the '--edit-key' command "minimize" before export except that the local copy of the key is not modified. Defaults to no.

--with-colons

> Print key listings delimited by colons. Note that the output will be encoded in UTF-8 regardless of any '--display-charset' setting. This format is useful when GnuPG is called from scripts and other programs as it is easily machine parsed. The details of this format are documented in the file 'doc/DETAILS', which is included in the GnuPG source distribution.

--print-pka-records

> Modify the output of the list commands to print PKA records suitable to put into DNS zone files. An ORIGIN line is printed before each record to allow diverting the records to the corresponding zone file.

--print-dane-records

> Modify the output of the list commands to print OpenPGP DANE records suitable to put into DNS zone files. An ORIGIN line is printed before each record to allow diverting the records to the corresponding zone file.

--fixed-list-mode

> Do not merge primary user ID and primary key in '--with-colon' listing mode and print all timestamps as seconds since 1970-01-01. Since GnuPG 2.0.10, this mode is always used and thus this option is obsolete; it does not harm to use it though.

--legacy-list-mode

> Revert to the pre-2.1 public key list mode. This only affects the human readable output and not the machine interface (i.e. --with-colons). Note that the legacy format does not allow to convey suitable information for elliptic curves.

--with-fingerprint

> Same as the command '--fingerprint' but changes only the format of the output and may be used together with another command.

--with-icao-spelling

> Print the ICAO spelling of the fingerprint in addition to the hex digits.

--with-keygrip

> Include the keygrip in the key listings.

--with-secret

> Include info about the presence of a secret key in public key listings done with --with-colons.

4.2.4 OpenPGP protocol specific options.

`-t, --textmode`
`--no-textmode`

> Treat input files as text and store them in the OpenPGP canonical text form with standard "CRLF" line endings. This also sets the necessary flags to inform the recipient that the encrypted or signed data is text and may need its line endings converted back to whatever the local system uses. This option is useful when communicating between two platforms that have different line ending conventions (UNIX-like to Mac, Mac to Windows, etc). '`--no-textmode`' disables this option, and is the default.

`--force-v3-sigs`
`--no-force-v3-sigs`
`--force-v4-certs`
`--no-force-v4-certs`

> These options are obsolete and have no effect since GnuPG 2.1.

`--force-mdc`

> Force the use of encryption with a modification detection code. This is always used with the newer ciphers (those with a blocksize greater than 64 bits), or if all of the recipient keys indicate MDC support in their feature flags.

`--disable-mdc`

> Disable the use of the modification detection code. Note that by using this option, the encrypted message becomes vulnerable to a message modification attack.

`--personal-cipher-preferences string`

> Set the list of personal cipher preferences to **string**. Use **gpg2--version** to get a list of available algorithms, and use **none** to set no preference at all. This allows the user to safely override the algorithm chosen by the recipient key preferences, as GPG will only select an algorithm that is usable by all recipients. The most highly ranked cipher in this list is also used for the '`--symmetric`' encryption command.

`--personal-digest-preferences string`

> Set the list of personal digest preferences to **string**. Use **gpg2--version** to get a list of available algorithms, and use **none** to set no preference at all. This allows the user to safely override the algorithm chosen by the recipient key preferences, as GPG will only select an algorithm that is usable by all recipients. The most highly ranked digest algorithm in this list is also used when signing without encryption (e.g. '`--clearsign`' or '`--sign`').

`--personal-compress-preferences string`

> Set the list of personal compression preferences to **string**. Use **gpg2--version** to get a list of available algorithms, and use **none** to set no preference at all. This allows the user to safely override the algorithm chosen by the recipient key preferences, as GPG will only select an algorithm that is usable by all recipients. The most highly ranked compression algorithm in this list is also used when there are no recipient keys to consider (e.g. '`--symmetric`').

--s2k-cipher-algo name

Use **name** as the cipher algorithm used to protect secret keys. The default cipher is AES-128. This cipher is also used for symmetric encryption with a passphrase if '--personal-cipher-preferences' and '--cipher-algo' is not given.

--s2k-digest-algo name

Use **name** as the digest algorithm used to mangle the passphrases. The default algorithm is SHA-1.

--s2k-mode n

Selects how passphrases are mangled. If **n** is 0 a plain passphrase (which is not recommended) will be used, a 1 adds a salt to the passphrase and a 3 (the default) iterates the whole process a number of times (see –s2k-count). Unless '--rfc1991' is used, this mode is also used for symmetric encryption with a passphrase.

--s2k-count n

Specify how many times the passphrase mangling is repeated. This value may range between 1024 and 65011712 inclusive. The default is inquired from gpg-agent. Note that not all values in the 1024-65011712 range are legal and if an illegal value is selected, GnuPG will round up to the nearest legal value. This option is only meaningful if '--s2k-mode' is 3.

4.2.5 Compliance options

These options control what GnuPG is compliant to. Only one of these options may be active at a time. Note that the default setting of this is nearly always the correct one. See the INTEROPERABILITY WITH OTHER OPENPGP PROGRAMS section below before using one of these options.

--gnupg   Use standard GnuPG behavior. This is essentially OpenPGP behavior (see '--openpgp'), but with some additional workarounds for common compatibility problems in different versions of PGP. This is the default option, so it is not generally needed, but it may be useful to override a different compliance option in the gpg.conf file.

--openpgp

Reset all packet, cipher and digest options to strict OpenPGP behavior. Use this option to reset all previous options like '--s2k-*', '--cipher-algo', '--digest-algo' and '--compress-algo' to OpenPGP compliant values. All PGP workarounds are disabled.

--rfc4880

Reset all packet, cipher and digest options to strict RFC-4880 behavior. Note that this is currently the same thing as '--openpgp'.

--rfc2440

Reset all packet, cipher and digest options to strict RFC-2440 behavior.

--rfc1991

Try to be more RFC-1991 (PGP 2.x) compliant. This option is deprecated will be removed in GnuPG 2.1.

--pgp2   Set up all options to be as PGP 2.x compliant as possible, and warn if an action is taken (e.g. encrypting to a non-RSA key) that will create a message that PGP 2.x will not be able to handle. Note that 'PGP 2.x' here means 'MIT PGP 2.6.2'. There are other versions of PGP 2.x available, but the MIT release is a good common baseline.

This option implies '`--rfc1991 --disable-mdc --no-force-v4-certs --escape-from-lines --force-v3-sigs --allow-weak-digest-algos --cipher-algo IDEA --digest-algo MD5 --compress-algo ZIP`'. It also disables '`--textmode`' when encrypting.

This option is deprecated will be removed in GnuPG 2.1. The reason for dropping PGP-2 support is that the PGP 2 format is not anymore considered safe (for example due to the use of the broken MD5 algorithm). Note that the decryption of PGP-2 created messages will continue to work.

--pgp6   Set up all options to be as PGP 6 compliant as possible. This restricts you to the ciphers IDEA (if the IDEA plugin is installed), 3DES, and CAST5, the hashes MD5, SHA1 and RIPEMD160, and the compression algorithms none and ZIP. This also disables –throw-keyids, and making signatures with signing subkeys as PGP 6 does not understand signatures made by signing subkeys.

This option implies '`--disable-mdc --escape-from-lines`'.

--pgp7   Set up all options to be as PGP 7 compliant as possible. This is identical to '`--pgp6`' except that MDCs are not disabled, and the list of allowable ciphers is expanded to add AES128, AES192, AES256, and TWOFISH.

--pgp8   Set up all options to be as PGP 8 compliant as possible. PGP 8 is a lot closer to the OpenPGP standard than previous versions of PGP, so all this does is disable '`--throw-keyids`' and set '`--escape-from-lines`'. All algorithms are allowed except for the SHA224, SHA384, and SHA512 digests.

4.2.6 Doing things one usually doesn't want to do.

-n
--dry-run
             Don't make any changes (this is not completely implemented).

--list-only
             Changes the behaviour of some commands. This is like '`--dry-run`' but different in some cases. The semantic of this command may be extended in the future. Currently it only skips the actual decryption pass and therefore enables a fast listing of the encryption keys.

-i
--interactive
             Prompt before overwriting any files.

--debug-level *level*
             Select the debug level for investigating problems. *level* may be a numeric value or by a keyword:

             none   No debugging at all. A value of less than 1 may be used instead of the keyword.

basic   Some basic debug messages. A value between 1 and 2 may be used
                instead of the keyword.

advanced   More verbose debug messages. A value between 3 and 5 may be
                used instead of the keyword.

expert   Even more detailed messages. A value between 6 and 8 may be
                used instead of the keyword.

guru   All of the debug messages you can get. A value greater than 8 may
                be used instead of the keyword. The creation of hash tracing files
                is only enabled if the keyword is used.

How these messages are mapped to the actual debugging flags is not specified
and may change with newer releases of this program. They are however carefully
selected to best aid in debugging.

--debug *flags*

Set debugging flags. All flags are or-ed and *flags* may be given in C syntax
(e.g. 0x0042) or as a comma separated list of flag names. To get a list of all
supported flags the single word "help" can be used.

--debug-all

Set all useful debugging flags.

--debug-iolbf

Set stdout into line buffered mode. This option is only honored when given on
the command line.

--faked-system-time *epoch*

This option is only useful for testing; it sets the system time back or forth to
epoch which is the number of seconds elapsed since the year 1970. Alternatively
epoch may be given as a full ISO time string (e.g. "20070924T154812").

--enable-progress-filter

Enable certain PROGRESS status outputs. This option allows frontends to
display a progress indicator while gpg is processing larger files. There is a
slight performance overhead using it.

--status-fd n

Write special status strings to the file descriptor n. See the file DETAILS in
the documentation for a listing of them.

--status-file file

Same as '--status-fd', except the status data is written to file **file**.

--logger-fd n

Write log output to file descriptor **n** and not to STDERR.

--log-file file
--logger-file file

Same as '--logger-fd', except the logger data is written to file **file**. Note
that '--log-file' is only implemented for GnuPG-2.

`--attribute-fd n`

> Write attribute subpackets to the file descriptor **n**. This is most useful for use with '`--status-fd`', since the status messages are needed to separate out the various subpackets from the stream delivered to the file descriptor.

`--attribute-file file`

> Same as '`--attribute-fd`', except the attribute data is written to file **file**.

`--comment string`
`--no-comments`

> Use **string** as a comment string in clear text signatures and ASCII armored messages or keys (see '`--armor`'). The default behavior is not to use a comment string. '`--comment`' may be repeated multiple times to get multiple comment strings. '`--no-comments`' removes all comments. It is a good idea to keep the length of a single comment below 60 characters to avoid problems with mail programs wrapping such lines. Note that comment lines, like all other header lines, are not protected by the signature.

`--emit-version`
`--no-emit-version`

> Force inclusion of the version string in ASCII armored output. If given once only the name of the program and the major number is emitted (default), given twice the minor is also emitted, given triple the micro is added, and given quad an operating system identification is also emitted. '`--no-emit-version`' disables the version line.

`--sig-notation name=value`
`--cert-notation name=value`
`-N, --set-notation name=value`

> Put the name value pair into the signature as notation data. **name** must consist only of printable characters or spaces, and must contain a '`@`' character in the form keyname@domain.example.com (substituting the appropriate keyname and domain name, of course). This is to help prevent pollution of the IETF reserved notation namespace. The '`--expert`' flag overrides the '`@`' check. **value** may be any printable string; it will be encoded in UTF8, so you should check that your '`--display-charset`' is set correctly. If you prefix **name** with an exclamation mark (!), the notation data will be flagged as critical (rfc4880:5.2.3.16). '`--sig-notation`' sets a notation for data signatures. '`--cert-notation`' sets a notation for key signatures (certifications). '`--set-notation`' sets both.
>
> There are special codes that may be used in notation names. "%k" will be expanded into the key ID of the key being signed, "%K" into the long key ID of the key being signed, "%f" into the fingerprint of the key being signed, "%s" into the key ID of the key making the signature, "%S" into the long key ID of the key making the signature, "%g" into the fingerprint of the key making the signature (which might be a subkey), "%p" into the fingerprint of the primary key of the key making the signature, "%c" into the signature count from the OpenPGP smartcard, and "%%" results in a single "%". %k, %K, and %f are

only meaningful when making a key signature (certification), and %c is only meaningful when using the OpenPGP smartcard.

`--sig-policy-url string`
`--cert-policy-url string`
`--set-policy-url string`

Use **string** as a Policy URL for signatures (rfc4880:5.2.3.20). If you prefix it with an exclamation mark (!), the policy URL packet will be flagged as critical. '`--sig-policy-url`' sets a policy url for data signatures. '`--cert-policy-url`' sets a policy url for key signatures (certifications). '`--set-policy-url`' sets both.

The same %-expandos used for notation data are available here as well.

`--sig-keyserver-url string`

Use **string** as a preferred keyserver URL for data signatures. If you prefix it with an exclamation mark (!), the keyserver URL packet will be flagged as critical.

The same %-expandos used for notation data are available here as well.

`--set-filename string`

Use **string** as the filename which is stored inside messages. This overrides the default, which is to use the actual filename of the file being encrypted. Using the empty string for *string* effectively removes the filename from the output.

`--for-your-eyes-only`
`--no-for-your-eyes-only`

Set the 'for your eyes only' flag in the message. This causes GnuPG to refuse to save the file unless the '`--output`' option is given, and PGP to use a "secure viewer" with a claimed Tempest-resistant font to display the message. This option overrides '`--set-filename`'. '`--no-for-your-eyes-only`' disables this option.

`--use-embedded-filename`
`--no-use-embedded-filename`

Try to create a file with a name as embedded in the data. This can be a dangerous option as it allows to overwrite files. Defaults to no.

`--cipher-algo name`

Use **name** as cipher algorithm. Running the program with the command '`--version`' yields a list of supported algorithms. If this is not used the cipher algorithm is selected from the preferences stored with the key. In general, you do not want to use this option as it allows you to violate the OpenPGP standard. '`--personal-cipher-preferences`' is the safe way to accomplish the same thing.

`--digest-algo name`

Use **name** as the message digest algorithm. Running the program with the command '`--version`' yields a list of supported algorithms. In general, you do not want to use this option as it allows you to violate the OpenPGP standard. '`--personal-digest-preferences`' is the safe way to accomplish the same thing.

`--compress-algo name`

> Use compression algorithm `name`. "zlib" is RFC-1950 ZLIB compression. "zip" is RFC-1951 ZIP compression which is used by PGP. "bzip2" is a more modern compression scheme that can compress some things better than zip or zlib, but at the cost of more memory used during compression and decompression. "uncompressed" or "none" disables compression. If this option is not used, the default behavior is to examine the recipient key preferences to see which algorithms the recipient supports. If all else fails, ZIP is used for maximum compatibility.
>
> ZLIB may give better compression results than ZIP, as the compression window size is not limited to 8k. BZIP2 may give even better compression results than that, but will use a significantly larger amount of memory while compressing and decompressing. This may be significant in low memory situations. Note, however, that PGP (all versions) only supports ZIP compression. Using any algorithm other than ZIP or "none" will make the message unreadable with PGP. In general, you do not want to use this option as it allows you to violate the OpenPGP standard. '`--personal-compress-preferences`' is the safe way to accomplish the same thing.

`--cert-digest-algo name`

> Use `name` as the message digest algorithm used when signing a key. Running the program with the command '`--version`' yields a list of supported algorithms. Be aware that if you choose an algorithm that GnuPG supports but other OpenPGP implementations do not, then some users will not be able to use the key signatures you make, or quite possibly your entire key.

`--disable-cipher-algo name`

> Never allow the use of `name` as cipher algorithm. The given name will not be checked so that a later loaded algorithm will still get disabled.

`--disable-pubkey-algo name`

> Never allow the use of `name` as public key algorithm. The given name will not be checked so that a later loaded algorithm will still get disabled.

`--throw-keyids`
`--no-throw-keyids`

> Do not put the recipient key IDs into encrypted messages. This helps to hide the receivers of the message and is a limited countermeasure against traffic analysis.[1] On the receiving side, it may slow down the decryption process because all available secret keys must be tried. '`--no-throw-keyids`' disables this option. This option is essentially the same as using '`--hidden-recipient`' for all recipients.

`--not-dash-escaped`

> This option changes the behavior of cleartext signatures so that they can be used for patch files. You should not send such an armored file via email because all spaces and line endings are hashed too. You can not use this option for data

---

[1] Using a little social engineering anyone who is able to decrypt the message can check whether one of the other recipients is the one he suspects.

which has 5 dashes at the beginning of a line, patch files don't have this. A special armor header line tells GnuPG about this cleartext signature option.

`--escape-from-lines`
`--no-escape-from-lines`

> Because some mailers change lines starting with "From " to ">From " it is good to handle such lines in a special way when creating cleartext signatures to prevent the mail system from breaking the signature. Note that all other PGP versions do it this way too. Enabled by default. '`--no-escape-from-lines`' disables this option.

`--passphrase-repeat n`

> Specify how many times **gpg2** will request a new passphrase be repeated. This is useful for helping memorize a passphrase. Defaults to 1 repetition.

`--passphrase-fd n`

> Read the passphrase from file descriptor **n**. Only the first line will be read from file descriptor **n**. If you use 0 for **n**, the passphrase will be read from STDIN. This can only be used if only one passphrase is supplied.
>
> Note that this passphrase is only used if the option '`--batch`' has also been given. This is different from GnuPG version 1.x.

`--passphrase-file file`

> Read the passphrase from file **file**. Only the first line will be read from file **file**. This can only be used if only one passphrase is supplied. Obviously, a passphrase stored in a file is of questionable security if other users can read this file. Don't use this option if you can avoid it. Note that this passphrase is only used if the option '`--batch`' has also been given. This is different from GnuPG version 1.x.

`--passphrase string`

> Use **string** as the passphrase. This can only be used if only one passphrase is supplied. Obviously, this is of very questionable security on a multi-user system. Don't use this option if you can avoid it. Note that this passphrase is only used if the option '`--batch`' has also been given. This is different from GnuPG version 1.x.

`--pinentry-mode mode`

> Set the pinentry mode to **mode**. Allowed values for **mode** are:
>
> | | |
> |---|---|
> | default | Use the default of the agent, which is **ask**. |
> | ask | Force the use of the Pinentry. |
> | cancel | Emulate use of Pinentry's cancel button. |
> | error | Return a Pinentry error ("No Pinentry"). |
> | loopback | Redirect Pinentry queries to the caller. Note that in contrast to Pinentry the user is not prompted again if he enters a bad password. |

`--command-fd n`

> This is a replacement for the deprecated shared-memory IPC mode. If this option is enabled, user input on questions is not expected from the TTY but

from the given file descriptor. It should be used together with '--status-fd'.
See the file doc/DETAILS in the source distribution for details on how to use
it.

--command-file file

> Same as '--command-fd', except the commands are read out of file file

--allow-non-selfsigned-uid
--no-allow-non-selfsigned-uid

> Allow the import and use of keys with user IDs which are not self-signed.
> This is not recommended, as a non self-signed user ID is trivial to forge.
> '--no-allow-non-selfsigned-uid' disables.

--allow-freeform-uid

> Disable all checks on the form of the user ID while generating a new one. This
> option should only be used in very special environments as it does not ensure
> the de-facto standard format of user IDs.

--ignore-time-conflict

> GnuPG normally checks that the timestamps associated with keys and signa-
> tures have plausible values. However, sometimes a signature seems to be older
> than the key due to clock problems. This option makes these checks just a
> warning. See also '--ignore-valid-from' for timestamp issues on subkeys.

--ignore-valid-from

> GnuPG normally does not select and use subkeys created in the future. This
> option allows the use of such keys and thus exhibits the pre-1.0.7 behaviour.
> You should not use this option unless there is some clock problem. See also
> '--ignore-time-conflict' for timestamp issues with signatures.

--ignore-crc-error

> The ASCII armor used by OpenPGP is protected by a CRC checksum against
> transmission errors. Occasionally the CRC gets mangled somewhere on
> the transmission channel but the actual content (which is protected by the
> OpenPGP protocol anyway) is still okay. This option allows GnuPG to ignore
> CRC errors.

--ignore-mdc-error

> This option changes a MDC integrity protection failure into a warning. This
> can be useful if a message is partially corrupt, but it is necessary to get as
> much data as possible out of the corrupt message. However, be aware that a
> MDC protection failure may also mean that the message was tampered with
> intentionally by an attacker.

--allow-weak-digest-algos

> Signatures made with the broken MD5 algorithm are normally rejected with
> an "invalid digest algorithm" message. This option allows the verification of
> signatures made with such weak algorithms.

--no-default-keyring

> Do not add the default keyrings to the list of keyrings. Note that GnuPG will
> not operate without any keyrings, so if you use this option and do not provide

alternate keyrings via '--keyring' or '--secret-keyring', then GnuPG will still use the default public or secret keyrings.

--skip-verify

Skip the signature verification step. This may be used to make the decryption faster if the signature verification is not needed.

--with-key-data

Print key listings delimited by colons (like '--with-colons') and print the public key data.

--fast-list-mode

Changes the output of the list commands to work faster; this is achieved by leaving some parts empty. Some applications don't need the user ID and the trust information given in the listings. By using this options they can get a faster listing. The exact behaviour of this option may change in future versions. If you are missing some information, don't use this option.

--no-literal

This is not for normal use. Use the source to see for what it might be useful.

--set-filesize

This is not for normal use. Use the source to see for what it might be useful.

--show-session-key

Display the session key used for one message. See '--override-session-key' for the counterpart of this option.

We think that Key Escrow is a Bad Thing; however the user should have the freedom to decide whether to go to prison or to reveal the content of one specific message without compromising all messages ever encrypted for one secret key.

You can also use this option if you receive an encrypted message which is abusive or offensive, to prove to the administrators of the messaging system that the ciphertext transmitted corresponds to an inappropriate plaintext so they can take action against the offending user.

--override-session-key string

Don't use the public key but the session key **string**. The format of this string is the same as the one printed by '--show-session-key'. This option is normally not used but comes handy in case someone forces you to reveal the content of an encrypted message; using this option you can do this without handing out the secret key.

--ask-sig-expire
--no-ask-sig-expire

When making a data signature, prompt for an expiration time. If this option is not specified, the expiration time set via '--default-sig-expire' is used. '--no-ask-sig-expire' disables this option.

--default-sig-expire

The default expiration time to use for signature expiration. Valid values are "0" for no expiration, a number followed by the letter d (for days), w (for weeks), m (for months), or y (for years) (for example "2m" for two months, or "5y" for five years), or an absolute date in the form YYYY-MM-DD. Defaults to "0".

`--ask-cert-expire`
`--no-ask-cert-expire`

When making a key signature, prompt for an expiration time. If this option is not specified, the expiration time set via '`--default-cert-expire`' is used. '`--no-ask-cert-expire`' disables this option.

`--default-cert-expire`

The default expiration time to use for key signature expiration. Valid values are "0" for no expiration, a number followed by the letter d (for days), w (for weeks), m (for months), or y (for years) (for example "2m" for two months, or "5y" for five years), or an absolute date in the form YYYY-MM-DD. Defaults to "0".

`--allow-secret-key-import`

This is an obsolete option and is not used anywhere.

`--allow-multiple-messages`
`--no-allow-multiple-messages`

Allow processing of multiple OpenPGP messages contained in a single file or stream. Some programs that call GPG are not prepared to deal with multiple messages being processed together, so this option defaults to no. Note that versions of GPG prior to 1.4.7 always allowed multiple messages.

Warning: Do not use this option unless you need it as a temporary workaround!

`--enable-special-filenames`

This options enables a mode in which filenames of the form '`-&n`', where n is a non-negative decimal number, refer to the file descriptor n and not to a file with that name.

`--no-expensive-trust-checks`

Experimental use only.

`--preserve-permissions`

Don't change the permissions of a secret keyring back to user read/write only. Use this option only if you really know what you are doing.

`--default-preference-list string`

Set the list of default preferences to **string**. This preference list is used for new keys and becomes the default for "setpref" in the edit menu.

`--default-keyserver-url name`

Set the default keyserver URL to **name**. This keyserver will be used as the keyserver URL when writing a new self-signature on a key, which includes key generation and changing preferences.

`--list-config`

Display various internal configuration parameters of GnuPG. This option is intended for external programs that call GnuPG to perform tasks, and is thus not generally useful. See the file '`doc/DETAILS`' in the source distribution for the details of which configuration items may be listed. '--list-config' is only usable with '--with-colons' set.

--list-gcrypt-config

Display various internal configuration parameters of Libgcrypt.

--gpgconf-list

This command is similar to '--list-config' but in general only internally used by the gpgconf tool.

--gpgconf-test

This is more or less dummy action. However it parses the configuration file and returns with failure if the configuration file would prevent gpg from startup. Thus it may be used to run a syntax check on the configuration file.

4.2.7 Deprecated options

--show-photos
--no-show-photos

Causes   '--list-keys',   '--list-sigs',   '--list-public-keys', '--list-secret-keys', and verifying a signature to also display the photo ID attached to the key, if any. See also '--photo-viewer'. These options are deprecated. Use '--list-options [no-]show-photos' and/or '--verify-options [no-]show-photos' instead.

--show-keyring

Display the keyring name at the head of key listings to show which keyring a given key resides on. This option is deprecated: use '--list-options [no-]show-keyring' instead.

--always-trust

Identical to '--trust-model always'. This option is deprecated.

--show-notation
--no-show-notation

Show signature notations in the '--list-sigs' or '--check-sigs' listings as well as when verifying a signature with a notation in it. These options are deprecated. Use '--list-options [no-]show-notation' and/or '--verify-options [no-]show-notation' instead.

--show-policy-url
--no-show-policy-url

Show policy URLs in the '--list-sigs' or '--check-sigs' listings as well as when verifying a signature with a policy URL in it. These options are deprecated. Use '--list-options [no-]show-policy-url' and/or '--verify-options [no-]show-policy-url' instead.

4.3 Configuration files

There are a few configuration files to control certain aspects of gpg2's operation. Unless noted, they are expected in the current home directory (see [option –homedir], page 4).

‘gpg.conf’

>This is the standard configuration file read by **gpg2** on startup. It may contain any valid long option; the leading two dashes may not be entered and the option may not be abbreviated. This default name may be changed on the command line (see [gpg-option –options], page 49). You should backup this file.

Note that on larger installations, it is useful to put predefined files into the directory ‘/usr/local/etc/skel/.gnupg’ so that newly created users start up with a working configuration. For existing users a small helper script is provided to create these files (see Section 8.3 [addgnupghome], page 117).

For internal purposes **gpg2** creates and maintains a few other files; They all live in in the current home directory (see [option –homedir], page 4). Only the **gpg2** program may modify these files.

‘~/.gnupg/pubring.gpg’

>The public keyring. You should backup this file.

‘~/.gnupg/pubring.gpg.lock’

>The lock file for the public keyring.

‘~/.gnupg/pubring.kbx’

>The public keyring using a different format. This file is sharred with **gpgsm**. You should backup this file.

‘~/.gnupg/pubring.kbx.lock’

>The lock file for ‘pubring.kbx’.

‘~/.gnupg/secring.gpg’

>A secret keyring as used by GnuPG versions before 2.1. It is not used by GnuPG 2.1 and later.

‘~/.gnupg/.gpg-v21-migrated’

>File indicating that a migration to GnuPG 2.1 has been done.

‘~/.gnupg/trustdb.gpg’

>The trust database. There is no need to backup this file; it is better to backup the ownertrust values (see [option –export-ownertrust], page 38).

‘~/.gnupg/trustdb.gpg.lock’

>The lock file for the trust database.

‘~/.gnupg/random_seed’

>A file used to preserve the state of the internal random pool.

‘~/.gnupg/secring.gpg.lock’

>The lock file for the secret keyring.

‘~/.gnupg/openpgp-revocs.d/’

>This is the directory where gpg stores pre-generated revocation certificates. The file name corresponds to the OpenPGP fingerprint of the respective key. It is suggested to backup those certificates and if the primary private key is not stored on the disk to move them to an external storage device. Anyone who can access theses files is able to revoke the corresponding key. You may want

to print them out. You should backup all files in this directory and take care
to keep this backup closed away.

'/usr/local/share/gnupg/options.skel'
>   The skeleton options file.

'/usr/local/lib/gnupg/'
>   Default location for extensions.

Operation is further controlled by a few environment variables:

HOME   Used to locate the default home directory.

GNUPGHOME
>   If set directory used instead of "~/.gnupg".

GPG_AGENT_INFO
>   This variable was used by GnuPG versions before 2.1

PINENTRY_USER_DATA
>   This value is passed via gpg-agent to pinentry. It is useful to convey extra
>   information to a custom pinentry.

COLUMNS
LINES   Used to size some displays to the full size of the screen.

LANGUAGE
>   Apart from its use by GNU, it is used in the W32 version to override the
>   language selection done through the Registry. If used and set to a valid and
>   available language name (*langid*), the file with the translation is loaded from
>
>   *gpgdir*/`gnupg.nls/`*langid*`.mo`. Here *gpgdir* is the directory out of which the
>   gpg binary has been loaded. If it can't be loaded the Registry is tried and as
>   last resort the native Windows locale system is used.

4.4 Examples

gpg -se -r Bob file
>   sign and encrypt for user Bob

gpg --clearsign file
>   make a clear text signature

gpg -sb file
>   make a detached signature

gpg -u 0x12345678 -sb file
>   make a detached signature with the key 0x12345678

gpg --list-keys user_ID
>   show keys

gpg --fingerprint user_ID
>   show fingerprint

gpg –verify `pgpfile`
gpg –verify `sigfile`

> Verify the signature of the file but do not output the data. The second form is used for detached signatures, where `sigfile` is the detached signature (either ASCII armored or binary) and are the signed data; if this is not given, the name of the file holding the signed data is constructed by cutting off the extension (".asc" or ".sig") of `sigfile` or by asking the user for the filename.

RETURN VALUE

The program returns 0 if everything was fine, 1 if at least a signature was bad, and other error codes for fatal errors.

WARNINGS

Use a *good* password for your user account and a *good* passphrase to protect your secret key. This passphrase is the weakest part of the whole system. Programs to do dictionary attacks on your secret keyring are very easy to write and so you should protect your "~/.gnupg/" directory very well.

Keep in mind that, if this program is used over a network (telnet), it is *very* easy to spy out your passphrase!

If you are going to verify detached signatures, make sure that the program knows about it; either give both filenames on the command line or use '-' to specify STDIN.

INTEROPERABILITY WITH OTHER OPENPGP PROGRAMS

GnuPG tries to be a very flexible implementation of the OpenPGP standard. In particular, GnuPG implements many of the optional parts of the standard, such as the SHA-512 hash, and the ZLIB and BZIP2 compression algorithms. It is important to be aware that not all OpenPGP programs implement these optional algorithms and that by forcing their use via the '--cipher-algo', '--digest-algo', '--cert-digest-algo', or '--compress-algo' options in GnuPG, it is possible to create a perfectly valid OpenPGP message, but one that cannot be read by the intended recipient.

There are dozens of variations of OpenPGP programs available, and each supports a slightly different subset of these optional algorithms. For example, until recently, no (unhacked) version of PGP supported the BLOWFISH cipher algorithm. A message using BLOWFISH simply could not be read by a PGP user. By default, GnuPG uses the standard OpenPGP preferences system that will always do the right thing and create messages that are usable by all recipients, regardless of which OpenPGP program they use. Only override this safe default if you really know what you are doing.

If you absolutely must override the safe default, or if the preferences on a given key are invalid for some reason, you are far better off using the '--pgp6', '--pgp7', or '--pgp8' options. These options are safe as they do not force any particular algorithms in violation of OpenPGP, but rather reduce the available algorithms to a "PGP-safe" list.

BUGS

On older systems this program should be installed as setuid(root). This is necessary to lock memory pages. Locking memory pages prevents the operating system from writing memory pages (which may contain passphrases or other sensitive material) to disk. If you get no warning message about insecure memory your operating system supports locking without being root. The program drops root privileges as soon as locked memory is allocated.

Note also that some systems (especially laptops) have the ability to "suspend to disk" (also known as "safe sleep" or "hibernate"). This writes all memory to disk before going into a low power or even powered off mode. Unless measures are taken in the operating system to protect the saved memory, passphrases or other sensitive material may be recoverable from it later.

Before you report a bug you should first search the mailing list archives for similar problems and second check whether such a bug has already been reported to our bug tracker at http://bugs.gnupg.org .

4.5 Unattended Usage

gpg is often used as a backend engine by other software. To help with this a machine interface has been defined to have an unambiguous way to do this. The options '--status-fd' and '--batch' are almost always required for this.

4.5.1 Unattended key generation

The command '--gen-key' may be used along with the option '--batch' for unattended key generation. The parameters are either read from stdin or given as a file on the command line. The format of the parameter file is as follows:

- Text only, line length is limited to about 1000 characters.
- UTF-8 encoding must be used to specify non-ASCII characters.
- Empty lines are ignored.
- Leading and trailing while space is ignored.
- A hash sign as the first non white space character indicates a comment line.
- Control statements are indicated by a leading percent sign, the arguments are separated by white space from the keyword.
- Parameters are specified by a keyword, followed by a colon. Arguments are separated by white space.
- The first parameter must be 'Key-Type'; control statements may be placed anywhere.
- The order of the parameters does not matter except for 'Key-Type' which must be the first parameter. The parameters are only used for the generated keyblock (primary and subkeys); parameters from previous sets are not used. Some syntactically checks may be performed.
- Key generation takes place when either the end of the parameter file is reached, the next 'Key-Type' parameter is encountered or at the control statement '%commit' is encountered.

Control statements:

%echo *text*

> Print *text* as diagnostic.

%dry-run   Suppress actual key generation (useful for syntax checking).

%commit   Perform the key generation. Note that an implicit commit is done at the next
> Key-Type parameter.

%pubring *filename*
%secring *filename*

> Do not write the key to the default or commandline given keyring but to *file-name*. This must be given before the first commit to take place, duplicate specification of the same filename is ignored, the last filename before a commit is used. The filename is used until a new filename is used (at commit points) and all keys are written to that file. If a new filename is given, this file is created (and overwrites an existing one). For GnuPG versions prior to 2.1, both control statements must be given. For GnuPG 2.1 and later '`%secring`' is a no-op.

%ask-passphrase
%no-ask-passphrase

> This option is a no-op for GnuPG 2.1 and later.

%no-protection

> Using this option allows the creation of keys without any passphrase protection. This option is mainly intended for regression tests.

%transient-key

> If given the keys are created using a faster and a somewhat less secure random number generator. This option may be used for keys which are only used for a short time and do not require full cryptographic strength. It takes only effect if used together with the control statement '`%no-protection`'.

General Parameters:

Key-Type: *algo*

> Starts a new parameter block by giving the type of the primary key. The algorithm must be capable of signing. This is a required parameter. *algo* may either be an OpenPGP algorithm number or a string with the algorithm name. The special value '`default`' may be used for *algo* to create the default key type; in this case a '`Key-Usage`' shall not be given and '`default`' also be used for '`Subkey-Type`'.

Key-Length: *nbits*

> The requested length of the generated key in bits. The default is returned by running the command '`gpg2 --gpgconf-list`'.

Key-Grip: *hexstring*

> This is optional and used to generate a CSR or certificate for an already existing key. Key-Length will be ignored when given.

Key-Usage: *usage-list*

> Space or comma delimited list of key usages. Allowed values are '`encrypt`', '`sign`', and '`auth`'. This is used to generate the key flags. Please make sure

that the algorithm is capable of this usage. Note that OpenPGP requires that all primary keys are capable of certification, so no matter what usage is given here, the 'cert' flag will be on. If no 'Key-Usage' is specified and the 'Key-Type' is not 'default', all allowed usages for that particular algorithm are used; if it is not given but 'default' is used the usage will be 'sign'.

Subkey-Type: *algo*

This generates a secondary key (subkey). Currently only one subkey can be handled. See also 'Key-Type' above.

Subkey-Length: *nbits*

Length of the secondary key (subkey) in bits. The default is returned by running the command 'gpg2 --gpgconf-list'".

Subkey-Usage: *usage-list*

Key usage lists for a subkey; similar to 'Key-Usage'.

Passphrase: *string*

If you want to specify a passphrase for the secret key, enter it here. Default is to use the Pinentry dialog to ask for a passphrase.

Name-Real: *name*
Name-Comment: *comment*
Name-Email: *email*

The three parts of a user name. Remember to use UTF-8 encoding here. If you don't give any of them, no user ID is created.

Expire-Date: *iso-date* | (*number*[d | w | m | y])

Set the expiration date for the key (and the subkey). It may either be entered in ISO date format (e.g. "20000815T145012") or as number of days, weeks, month or years after the creation date. The special notation "seconds=N" is also allowed to specify a number of seconds since creation. Without a letter days are assumed. Note that there is no check done on the overflow of the type used by OpenPGP for timestamps. Thus you better make sure that the given value make sense. Although OpenPGP works with time intervals, GnuPG uses an absolute value internally and thus the last year we can represent is 2105.

Creation-Date: *iso-date*

Set the creation date of the key as stored in the key information and which is also part of the fingerprint calculation. Either a date like "1986-04-26" or a full timestamp like "19860426T042640" may be used. The time is considered to be UTC. The special notation "seconds=N" may be used to directly specify a the number of seconds since Epoch (Unix time). If it is not given the current time is used.

Preferences: *string*

Set the cipher, hash, and compression preference values for this key. This expects the same type of string as the sub-command 'setpref' in the '--edit-key' menu.

Revoker: *algo:fpr* [sensitive]

Add a designated revoker to the generated key. Algo is the public key algorithm of the designated revoker (i.e. RSA=1, DSA=17, etc.) *fpr* is the fingerprint of the designated revoker. The optional 'sensitive' flag marks the designated revoker as sensitive information. Only v4 keys may be designated revokers.

Keyserver: *string*

This is an optional parameter that specifies the preferred keyserver URL for the key.

Handle: *string*

This is an optional parameter only used with the status lines KEY_CREATED and KEY_NOT_CREATED. *string* may be up to 100 characters and should not contain spaces. It is useful for batch key generation to associate a key parameter block with a status line.

Here is an example on how to create a key:

```
$ cat >foo <<EOF
    %echo Generating a basic OpenPGP key
    Key-Type: DSA
    Key-Length: 1024
    Subkey-Type: ELG-E
    Subkey-Length: 1024
    Name-Real: Joe Tester
    Name-Comment: with stupid passphrase
    Name-Email: joe@foo.bar
    Expire-Date: 0
    Passphrase: abc
    %pubring foo.pub
    %secring foo.sec
    # Do a commit here, so that we can later print "done" :-)
    %commit
    %echo done
EOF
$ gpg2 --batch --gen-key foo
 [...]
$ gpg2 --no-default-keyring --secret-keyring ./foo.sec \
     --keyring ./foo.pub --list-secret-keys
/home/wk/work/gnupg-stable/scratch/foo.sec
------------------------------------------
sec  1024D/915A878D 2000-03-09 Joe Tester (with stupid passphrase) <joe@foo.bar>
ssb  1024g/8F70E2C0 2000-03-09
```

If you want to create a key with the default algorithms you would use these parameters:

```
    %echo Generating a default key
    Key-Type: default
    Subkey-Type: default
    Name-Real: Joe Tester
    Name-Comment: with stupid passphrase
    Name-Email: joe@foo.bar
    Expire-Date: 0
    Passphrase: abc
    %pubring foo.pub
    %secring foo.sec
    # Do a commit here, so that we can later print "done" :-)
    %commit
    %echo done
```

5 Invoking GPGSM

`gpgsm` is a tool similar to `gpg` to provide digital encryption and signing services on X.509 certificates and the CMS protocol. It is mainly used as a backend for S/MIME mail processing. `gpgsm` includes a full featured certificate management and complies with all rules defined for the German Sphinx project.

See [Option Index], page 167, for an index to GPGSM's commands and options.

5.1 Commands

Commands are not distinguished from options except for the fact that only one command is allowed.

5.1.1 Commands not specific to the function

`--version`

> Print the program version and licensing information. Note that you cannot abbreviate this command.

`--help, -h`

> Print a usage message summarizing the most useful command-line options. Note that you cannot abbreviate this command.

`--warranty`

> Print warranty information. Note that you cannot abbreviate this command.

`--dump-options`

> Print a list of all available options and commands. Note that you cannot abbreviate this command.

5.1.2 Commands to select the type of operation

`--encrypt`

> Perform an encryption. The keys the data is encrypted too must be set using the option '`--recipient`'.

`--decrypt`

> Perform a decryption; the type of input is automatically determined. It may either be in binary form or PEM encoded; automatic determination of base-64 encoding is not done.

`--sign`   Create a digital signature. The key used is either the fist one found in the keybox or those set with the '`--local-user`' option.

`--verify`   Check a signature file for validity. Depending on the arguments a detached signature may also be checked.

`--server`   Run in server mode and wait for commands on the `stdin`.

`--call-dirmngr` *command* [*args*]

> Behave as a Dirmngr client issuing the request *command* with the optional list of *args*. The output of the Dirmngr is printed stdout. Please note that file names given as arguments should have an absolute file name (i.e. commencing with /

because they are passed verbatim to the Dirmngr and the working directory of the Dirmngr might not be the same as the one of this client. Currently it is not possible to pass data via stdin to the Dirmngr. *command* should not contain spaces.

This is command is required for certain maintaining tasks of the dirmngr where a dirmngr must be able to call back to **gpgsm**. See the Dirmngr manual for details.

`--call-protect-tool` *arguments*

Certain maintenance operations are done by an external program call **gpg-protect-tool**; this is usually not installed in a directory listed in the PATH variable. This command provides a simple wrapper to access this tool. *arguments* are passed verbatim to this command; use '`--help`' to get a list of supported operations.

5.1.3 How to manage the certificates and keys

`--gen-key`

This command allows the creation of a certificate signing request or a self-signed certificate. It is commonly used along with the '`--output`' option to save the created CSR or certificate into a file. If used with the '`--batch`' a parameter file is used to create the CSR or certificate and it is further possible to create non-self-signed certificates.

`--list-keys`
`-k`   List all available certificates stored in the local key database. Note that the displayed data might be reformatted for better human readability and illegal characters are replaced by safe substitutes.

`--list-secret-keys`
`-K`   List all available certificates for which a corresponding a secret key is available.

`--list-external-keys` *pattern*

List certificates matching *pattern* using an external server. This utilizes the **dirmngr** service.

`--list-chain`

Same as '`--list-keys`' but also prints all keys making up the chain.

`--dump-cert`
`--dump-keys`

List all available certificates stored in the local key database using a format useful mainly for debugging.

`--dump-chain`

Same as '`--dump-keys`' but also prints all keys making up the chain.

`--dump-secret-keys`

List all available certificates for which a corresponding a secret key is available using a format useful mainly for debugging.

`--dump-external-keys` *pattern*

>   List certificates matching *pattern* using an external server. This utilizes the `dirmngr` service. It uses a format useful mainly for debugging.

`--keydb-clear-some-cert-flags`

>   This is a debugging aid to reset certain flags in the key database which are used to cache certain certificate stati. It is especially useful if a bad CRL or a weird running OCSP responder did accidentally revoke certificate. There is no security issue with this command because `gpgsm` always make sure that the validity of a certificate is checked right before it is used.

`--delete-keys` *pattern*

>   Delete the keys matching *pattern*. Note that there is no command to delete the secret part of the key directly. In case you need to do this, you should run the command `gpgsm --dump-secret-keys KEYID` before you delete the key, copy the string of hex-digits in the "keygrip" line and delete the file consisting of these hex-digits and the suffix `.key` from the 'private-keys-v1.d' directory below our GnuPG home directory (usually '~/.gnupg').

`--export [`*pattern*`]`

>   Export all certificates stored in the Keybox or those specified by the optional *pattern*. Those pattern consist of a list of user ids (see [how-to-specify-a-user-id], page 111). When used along with the '`--armor`' option a few informational lines are prepended before each block. There is one limitation: As there is no commonly agreed upon way to pack more than one certificate into an ASN.1 structure, the binary export (i.e. without using '`armor`') works only for the export of one certificate. Thus it is required to specify a *pattern* which yields exactly one certificate. Ephemeral certificate are only exported if all *pattern* are given as fingerprints or keygrips.

`--export-secret-key-p12` *key-id*

>   Export the private key and the certificate identified by *key-id* in a PKCS#12 format. When used with the `--armor` option a few informational lines are prepended to the output. Note, that the PKCS#12 format is not very secure and this command is only provided if there is no other way to exchange the private key. (see [option –p12-charset], page 87)

`--export-secret-key-p8` *key-id*
`--export-secret-key-raw` *key-id*

>   Export the private key of the certificate identified by *key-id* with any encryption stripped. The `...-raw` command exports in PKCS#1 format; the `...-p8` command exports in PKCS#8 format. When used with the `--armor` option a few informational lines are prepended to the output. These commands are useful to prepare a key for use on a TLS server.

`--import [`*files*`]`

>   Import the certificates from the PEM or binary encoded files as well as from signed-only messages. This command may also be used to import a secret key from a PKCS#12 file.

--learn-card

> Read information about the private keys from the smartcard and import the certificates from there. This command utilizes the **gpg-agent** and in turn the **scdaemon**.

--passwd *user_id*

> Change the passphrase of the private key belonging to the certificate specified as *user_id*. Note, that changing the passphrase/PIN of a smartcard is not yet supported.

5.2 Option Summary

GPGSM features a bunch of options to control the exact behaviour and to change the default configuration.

5.2.1 How to change the configuration

These options are used to change the configuration and are usually found in the option file.

--options *file*

> Reads configuration from *file* instead of from the default per-user configuration file. The default configuration file is named 'gpgsm.conf' and expected in the '.gnupg' directory directly below the home directory of the user.

--homedir *dir*

> Set the name of the home directory to *dir*. If this option is not used, the home directory defaults to '~/.gnupg'. It is only recognized when given on the command line. It also overrides any home directory stated through the environment variable GNUPGHOME or (on Windows systems) by means of the Registry entry *HKCU\Software\GNU\GnuPG:HomeDir*.
>
> On Windows systems it is possible to install GnuPG as a portable application. In this case only this command line option is considered, all other ways to set a home directory are ignored.
>
> To install GnuPG as a portable application under Windows, create an empty file name 'gpgconf.ctl' in the same directory as the tool 'gpgconf.exe'. The root of the installation is than that directory; or, if 'gpgconf.exe' has been installed directly below a directory named 'bin', its parent directory. You also need to make sure that the following directories exist and are writable: 'ROOT/home' for the GnuPG home and 'ROOT/usr/local/var/cache/gnupg' for internal cache files.

-v

--verbose

> Outputs additional information while running. You can increase the verbosity by giving several verbose commands to **gpgsm**, such as '-vv'.

--policy-file *filename*

> Change the default name of the policy file to *filename*.

--agent-program *file*

> Specify an agent program to be used for secret key operations. The default value is determined by running the command **gpgconf**. Note that the pipe

symbol (|) is used for a regression test suite hack and may thus not be used in the file name.

`--dirmngr-program` *file*

Specify a dirmngr program to be used for CRL checks. The default value is '/usr/local/bin/dirmngr'. This is only used as a fallback when the environment variable `DIRMNGR_INFO` is not set or a running dirmngr cannot be connected.

`--prefer-system-dirmngr`

If a system wide `dirmngr` is running in daemon mode, first try to connect to this one. Fallback to a pipe based server if this does not work. Under Windows this option is ignored because the system dirmngr is always used.

`--disable-dirmngr`

Entirely disable the use of the Dirmngr.

`--no-autostart`

Do not start the gpg-agent or the dirmngr if it has not yet been started and its service is required. This option is mostly useful on machines where the connection to gpg-agent has been redirected to another machines. If dirmngr is required on the remote machine, it may be started manually using **gpgconf** **--launch dirmngr**.

`--no-secmem-warning`

Do not print a warning when the so called "secure memory" cannot be used.

`--log-file` *file*

When running in server mode, append all logging output to *file*.

5.2.2 Certificate related options

`--enable-policy-checks`
`--disable-policy-checks`

By default policy checks are enabled. These options may be used to change it.

`--enable-crl-checks`
`--disable-crl-checks`

By default the CRL checks are enabled and the DirMngr is used to check for revoked certificates. The disable option is most useful with an off-line network connection to suppress this check.

`--enable-trusted-cert-crl-check`
`--disable-trusted-cert-crl-check`

By default the CRL for trusted root certificates are checked like for any other certificates. This allows a CA to revoke its own certificates voluntary without the need of putting all ever issued certificates into a CRL. The disable option may be used to switch this extra check off. Due to the caching done by the Dirmngr, there will not be any noticeable performance gain. Note, that this also disables possible OCSP checks for trusted root certificates. A more specific way of disabling this check is by adding the "relax" keyword to the root CA line of the 'trustlist.txt'

`--force-crl-refresh`

>Tell the dirmngr to reload the CRL for each request. For better performance, the dirmngr will actually optimize this by suppressing the loading for short time intervals (e.g. 30 minutes). This option is useful to make sure that a fresh CRL is available for certificates hold in the keybox. The suggested way of doing this is by using it along with the option '`--with-validation`' for a key listing command. This option should not be used in a configuration file.

`--enable-ocsp`
`--disable-ocsp`

>By default OCSP checks are disabled. The enable option may be used to enable OCSP checks via Dirmngr. If CRL checks are also enabled, CRLs will be used as a fallback if for some reason an OCSP request will not succeed. Note, that you have to allow OCSP requests in Dirmngr's configuration too (option '`--allow-ocsp`') and configure Dirmngr properly. If you do not do so you will get the error code '`Not supported`'.

`--auto-issuer-key-retrieve`

>If a required certificate is missing while validating the chain of certificates, try to load that certificate from an external location. This usually means that Dirmngr is employed to search for the certificate. Note that this option makes a "web bug" like behavior possible. LDAP server operators can see which keys you request, so by sending you a message signed by a brand new key (which you naturally will not have on your local keybox), the operator can tell both your IP address and the time when you verified the signature.

`--validation-model` *name*

>This option changes the default validation model. The only possible values are "shell" (which is the default), "chain" which forces the use of the chain model and "steed" for a new simplified model. The chain model is also used if an option in the '`trustlist.txt`' or an attribute of the certificate requests it. However the standard model (shell) is in that case always tried first.

`--ignore-cert-extension` *oid*

>Add *oid* to the list of ignored certificate extensions. The *oid* is expected to be in dotted decimal form, like `2.5.29.3`. This option may be used more than once. Critical flagged certificate extensions matching one of the OIDs in the list are treated as if they are actually handled and thus the certificate will not be rejected due to an unknown critical extension. Use this option with care because extensions are usually flagged as critical for a reason.

5.2.3 Input and Output

`--armor`
`-a`   Create PEM encoded output. Default is binary output.

`--base64`   Create Base-64 encoded output; i.e. PEM without the header lines.

`--assume-armor`

>Assume the input data is PEM encoded. Default is to autodetect the encoding but this is may fail.

`--assume-base64`

> Assume the input data is plain base-64 encoded.

`--assume-binary`

> Assume the input data is binary encoded.

`--p12-charset` *name*

> **gpgsm** uses the UTF-8 encoding when encoding passphrases for PKCS#12 files. This option may be used to force the passphrase to be encoded in the specified encoding *name*. This is useful if the application used to import the key uses a different encoding and thus will not be able to import a file generated by **gpgsm**. Commonly used values for *name* are **Latin1** and **CP850**. Note that **gpgsm** itself automagically imports any file with a passphrase encoded to the most commonly used encodings.

`--default-key` *user_id*

> Use *user_id* as the standard key for signing. This key is used if no other key has been defined as a signing key. Note, that the first '`--local-users`' option also sets this key if it has not yet been set; however '`--default-key`' always overrides this.

`--local-user` *user_id*
`-u` *user_id*

> Set the user(s) to be used for signing. The default is the first secret key found in the database.

`--recipient` *name*
`-r`

> Encrypt to the user id *name*. There are several ways a user id may be given (see [how-to-specify-a-user-id], page 111).

`--output` *file*
`-o` *file*   Write output to *file*. The default is to write it to stdout.

`--with-key-data`

> Displays extra information with the `--list-keys` commands. Especially a line tagged **grp** is printed which tells you the keygrip of a key. This string is for example used as the file name of the secret key.

`--with-validation`

> When doing a key listing, do a full validation check for each key and print the result. This is usually a slow operation because it requires a CRL lookup and other operations.
>
> When used along with –import, a validation of the certificate to import is done and only imported if it succeeds the test. Note that this does not affect an already available certificate in the DB. This option is therefore useful to simply verify a certificate.

`--with-md5-fingerprint`

> For standard key listings, also print the MD5 fingerprint of the certificate.

`--with-keygrip`

> Include the keygrip in standard key listings. Note that the keygrip is always listed in –with-colons mode.

`--with-secret`
> Include info about the presence of a secret key in public key listings done with `--with-colons`.

5.2.4 How to change how the CMS is created.

`--include-certs n`
> Using *n* of -2 includes all certificate except for the root cert, -1 includes all certs, 0 does not include any certs, 1 includes only the signers cert and all other positive values include up to *n* certificates starting with the signer cert. The default is -2.

`--cipher-algo oid`
> Use the cipher algorithm with the ASN.1 object identifier *oid* for encryption. For convenience the strings 3DES, AES and AES256 may be used instead of their OIDs. The default is AES (2.16.840.1.101.3.4.1.2).

`--digest-algo name`
> Use name as the message digest algorithm. Usually this algorithm is deduced from the respective signing certificate. This option forces the use of the given algorithm and may lead to severe interoperability problems.

5.2.5 Doing things one usually do not want to do.

`--extra-digest-algo name`
> Sometimes signatures are broken in that they announce a different digest algorithm than actually used. gpgsm uses a one-pass data processing model and thus needs to rely on the announced digest algorithms to properly hash the data. As a workaround this option may be used to tell gpg to also hash the data using the algorithm *name*; this slows processing down a little bit but allows to verify such broken signatures. If gpgsm prints an error like "digest algo 8 has not been enabled" you may want to try this option, with 'SHA256' for *name*.

`--faked-system-time epoch`
> This option is only useful for testing; it sets the system time back or forth to *epoch* which is the number of seconds elapsed since the year 1970. Alternatively *epoch* may be given as a full ISO time string (e.g. "20070924T154812").

`--with-ephemeral-keys`
> Include ephemeral flagged keys in the output of key listings. Note that they are included anyway if the key specification for a listing is given as fingerprint or keygrip.

`--debug-level level`
> Select the debug level for investigating problems. *level* may be a numeric value or by a keyword:

> none   No debugging at all. A value of less than 1 may be used instead of the keyword.

> basic   Some basic debug messages. A value between 1 and 2 may be used instead of the keyword.

advanced   More verbose debug messages. A value between 3 and 5 may be used instead of the keyword.

expert   Even more detailed messages. A value between 6 and 8 may be used instead of the keyword.

guru   All of the debug messages you can get. A value greater than 8 may be used instead of the keyword. The creation of hash tracing files is only enabled if the keyword is used.

How these messages are mapped to the actual debugging flags is not specified and may change with newer releases of this program. They are however carefully selected to best aid in debugging.

`--debug` *flags*

This option is only useful for debugging and the behaviour may change at any time without notice; using `--debug-levels` is the preferred method to select the debug verbosity. FLAGS are bit encoded and may be given in usual C-Syntax. The currently defined bits are:

0 (1)   X.509 or OpenPGP protocol related data

1 (2)   values of big number integers

2 (4)   low level crypto operations

5 (32)   memory allocation

6 (64)   caching

7 (128)   show memory statistics.

9 (512)   write hashed data to files named `dbgmd-000*`

10 (1024)   trace Assuan protocol

Note, that all flags set using this option may get overridden by `--debug-level`.

`--debug-all`

Same as `--debug=0xffffffff`

`--debug-allow-core-dump`

Usually **gpgsm** tries to avoid dumping core by well written code and by disabling core dumps for security reasons. However, bugs are pretty durable beasts and to squash them it is sometimes useful to have a core dump. This option enables core dumps unless the Bad Thing happened before the option parsing.

`--debug-no-chain-validation`

This is actually not a debugging option but only useful as such. It lets **gpgsm** bypass all certificate chain validation checks.

`--debug-ignore-expiration`

This is actually not a debugging option but only useful as such. It lets **gpgsm** ignore all notAfter dates, this is used by the regression tests.

`--fixed-passphrase` *string*

Supply the passphrase *string* to the gpg-protect-tool. This option is only useful for the regression tests included with this package and may be revised or removed at any time without notice.

`--no-common-certs-import`

Suppress the import of common certificates on keybox creation.

All the long options may also be given in the configuration file after stripping off the two leading dashes.

5.3 Configuration files

There are a few configuration files to control certain aspects of **gpgsm**'s operation. Unless noted, they are expected in the current home directory (see [option –homedir], page 4).

'`gpgsm.conf`'

This is the standard configuration file read by **gpgsm** on startup. It may contain any valid long option; the leading two dashes may not be entered and the option may not be abbreviated. This default name may be changed on the command line (see [gpgsm-option –options], page 84). You should backup this file.

'`policies.txt`'

This is a list of allowed CA policies. This file should list the object identifiers of the policies line by line. Empty lines and lines starting with a hash mark are ignored. Policies missing in this file and not marked as critical in the certificate will print only a warning; certificates with policies marked as critical and not listed in this file will fail the signature verification. You should backup this file.

For example, to allow only the policy 2.289.9.9, the file should look like this:

```
# Allowed policies
2.289.9.9
```

'`qualified.txt`'

This is the list of root certificates used for qualified certificates. They are defined as certificates capable of creating legally binding signatures in the same way as handwritten signatures are. Comments start with a hash mark and empty lines are ignored. Lines do have a length limit but this is not a serious limitation as the format of the entries is fixed and checked by gpgsm: A non-comment line starts with optional whitespace, followed by exactly 40 hex character, white space and a lowercased 2 letter country code. Additional data delimited with by a white space is current ignored but might late be used for other purposes.

Note that even if a certificate is listed in this file, this does not mean that the certificate is trusted; in general the certificates listed in this file need to be listed also in '`trustlist.txt`'.

This is a global file an installed in the data directory (e.g. '`/usr/local/share/gnupg/qualified.txt`'). GnuPG installs a suitable file with root certificates as used in Germany. As new Root-CA certificates may be issued over time, these entries may need to be updated; new distributions of this software should come with an updated list but it is still the responsibility of the Administrator to check that this list is correct.

Everytime **gpgsm** uses a certificate for signing or verification this file will be consulted to check whether the certificate under question has ultimately been issued by one of these CAs. If this is the case the user will be informed that the verified signature represents a legally binding ("qualified") signature. When creating a signature using such a certificate an extra prompt will be issued to let the user confirm that such a legally binding signature shall really be created.

Because this software has not yet been approved for use with such certificates, appropriate notices will be shown to indicate this fact.

'help.txt'

This is plain text file with a few help entries used with pinentry as well as a large list of help items for gpg and gpgsm. The standard file has English help texts; to install localized versions use filenames like 'help.LL.txt' with LL denoting the locale. GnuPG comes with a set of predefined help files in the data directory (e.g. '/usr/local/share/gnupg/gnupg/help.de.txt') and allows overriding of any help item by help files stored in the system configuration directory (e.g. '/usr/local/etc/gnupg/help.de.txt'). For a reference of the help file's syntax, please see the installed 'help.txt' file.

'com-certs.pem'

This file is a collection of common certificates used to populated a newly created 'pubring.kbx'. An administrator may replace this file with a custom one. The format is a concatenation of PEM encoded X.509 certificates. This global file is installed in the data directory (e.g. '/usr/local/share/gnupg/com-certs.pem').

Note that on larger installations, it is useful to put predefined files into the directory '/etc/skel/.gnupg/' so that newly created users start up with a working configuration. For existing users a small helper script is provided to create these files (see Section 8.3 [addgnupghome], page 117).

For internal purposes gpgsm creates and maintains a few other files; they all live in in the current home directory (see [option --homedir], page 4). Only gpgsm may modify these files.

'pubring.kbx'

This a database file storing the certificates as well as meta information. For debugging purposes the tool kbxutil may be used to show the internal structure of this file. You should backup this file.

'random_seed'

This content of this file is used to maintain the internal state of the random number generator across invocations. The same file is used by other programs of this software too.

'S.gpg-agent'

If this file exists gpgsm will first try to connect to this socket for accessing gpg-agent before starting a new gpg-agent instance. Under Windows this socket (which in reality be a plain file describing a regular TCP listening port) is the standard way of connecting the gpg-agent.

5.4 Examples

```
$ gpgsm -er goo@bar.net <plaintext >ciphertext
```

5.5 Unattended Usage

gpgsm is often used as a backend engine by other software. To help with this a machine interface has been defined to have an unambiguous way to do this. This is most likely used with the --server command but may also be used in the standard operation mode by using the --status-fd option.

5.5.1 Automated signature checking

It is very important to understand the semantics used with signature verification. Checking a signature is not as simple as it may sound and so the operation is a bit complicated. In most cases it is required to look at several status lines. Here is a table of all cases a signed message may have:

The signature is valid

> This does mean that the signature has been successfully verified, the certificates are all sane. However there are two subcases with important information: One of the certificates may have expired or a signature of a message itself as expired. It is a sound practise to consider such a signature still as valid but additional information should be displayed. Depending on the subcase gpgsm will issue these status codes:

> signature valid and nothing did expire
> > GOODSIG, VALIDSIG, TRUST_FULLY

> signature valid but at least one certificate has expired
> > EXPKEYSIG, VALIDSIG, TRUST_FULLY

> signature valid but expired
> > EXPSIG, VALIDSIG, TRUST_FULLY Note, that this case is currently not implemented.

The signature is invalid

> This means that the signature verification failed (this is an indication of af a transfer error, a program error or tampering with the message). gpgsm issues one of these status codes sequences:

> BADSIG

> GOODSIG, VALIDSIG TRUST_NEVER

Error verifying a signature

> For some reason the signature could not be verified, i.e. it cannot be decided whether the signature is valid or invalid. A common reason for this is a missing certificate.

5.5.2 CSR and certificate creation

The command '--gen-key' may be used along with the option '--batch' to either create a certificate signing request (CSR) or an X.509 certificate. This is controlled by a parameter file; the format of this file is as follows:

- Text only, line length is limited to about 1000 characters.
- UTF-8 encoding must be used to specify non-ASCII characters.

- Empty lines are ignored.

- Leading and trailing while space is ignored.

- A hash sign as the first non white space character indicates a comment line.

- Control statements are indicated by a leading percent sign, the arguments are separated by white space from the keyword.

- Parameters are specified by a keyword, followed by a colon. Arguments are separated by white space.

- The first parameter must be 'Key-Type', control statements may be placed anywhere.

- The order of the parameters does not matter except for 'Key-Type' which must be the first parameter. The parameters are only used for the generated CSR/certificate; parameters from previous sets are not used. Some syntactically checks may be performed.

- Key generation takes place when either the end of the parameter file is reached, the next 'Key-Type' parameter is encountered or at the control statement '%commit' is encountered.

Control statements:

%echo *text*
> Print *text* as diagnostic.

%dry-run   Suppress actual key generation (useful for syntax checking).

%commit   Perform the key generation. Note that an implicit commit is done at the next Key-Type parameter.

General Parameters:

Key-Type: *algo*
> Starts a new parameter block by giving the type of the primary key. The algorithm must be capable of signing. This is a required parameter. The only supported value for *algo* is 'rsa'.

Key-Length: *nbits*
> The requested length of a generated key in bits. Defaults to 2048.

Key-Grip: *hexstring*
> This is optional and used to generate a CSR or certificatet for an already existing key. Key-Length will be ignored when given.

Key-Usage: *usage-list*
> Space or comma delimited list of key usage, allowed values are 'encrypt', 'sign' and 'cert'. This is used to generate the keyUsage extension. Please make sure that the algorithm is capable of this usage. Default is to allow encrypt and sign.

Name-DN: *subject-name*
> This is the Distinguished Name (DN) of the subject in RFC-2253 format.

Name-Email: *string*
> This is an email address for the altSubjectName. This parameter is optional but may occur several times to add several email addresses to a certificate.

Name-DNS: *string*

> The is an DNS name for the altSubjectName. This parameter is optional but may occur several times to add several DNS names to a certificate.

Name-URI: *string*

> This is an URI for the altSubjectName. This parameter is optional but may occur several times to add several URIs to a certificate.

Additional parameters used to create a certificate (in contrast to a certificate signing request):

Serial: *sn* If this parameter is given an X.509 certificate will be generated. *sn* is expected to be a hex string representing an unsigned integer of arbitary length. The special value 'random' can be used to create a 64 bit random serial number.

Issuer-DN: *issuer-name*

> This is the DN name of the issuer in rfc2253 format. If it is not set it will default to the subject DN and a special GnuPG extension will be included in the certificate to mark it as a standalone certificate.

Creation-Date: *iso-date*
Not-Before: *iso-date*

> Set the notBefore date of the certificate. Either a date like '1986-04-26' or '1986-04-26 12:00' or a standard ISO timestamp like '19860426T042640' may be used. The time is considered to be UTC. If it is not given the current date is used.

Expire-Date: *iso-date*
Not-After: *iso-date*

> Set the notAfter date of the certificate. Either a date like '2063-04-05' or '2063-04-05 17:00' or a standard ISO timestamp like '20630405T170000' may be used. The time is considered to be UTC. If it is not given a default value in the not too far future is used.

Signing-Key: *keygrip*

> This gives the keygrip of the key used to sign the certificate. If it is not given a self-signed certificate will be created. For compatibility with future versions, it is suggested to prefix the keygrip with a '&'.

Hash-Algo: *hash-algo*

> Use *hash-algo* for this CSR or certificate. The supported hash algorithms are: 'sha1', 'sha256', 'sha384' and 'sha512'; they may also be specified with uppercase letters. The default is 'sha256'.

5.6 The Protocol the Server Mode Uses.

Description of the protocol used to access GPGSM. GPGSM does implement the Assuan protocol and in addition provides a regular command line interface which exhibits a full client to this protocol (but uses internal linking). To start gpgsm as a server the command line the option --server must be used. Additional options are provided to select the communication method (i.e. the name of the socket).

We assume that the connection has already been established; see the Assuan manual for details.

5.6.1 Encrypting a Message

Before encryption can be done the recipient must be set using the command:

> RECIPIENT *userID*

Set the recipient for the encryption. *userID* should be the internal representation of the key; the server may accept any other way of specification. If this is a valid and trusted recipient the server does respond with OK, otherwise the return is an ERR with the reason why the recipient cannot be used, the encryption will then not be done for this recipient. If the policy is not to encrypt at all if not all recipients are valid, the client has to take care of this. All `RECIPIENT` commands are cumulative until a `RESET` or an successful `ENCRYPT` command.

> INPUT FD[=*n*] [--armor|--base64|--binary]

Set the file descriptor for the message to be encrypted to *n*. Obviously the pipe must be open at that point, the server establishes its own end. If the server returns an error the client should consider this session failed. If *n* is not given, this commands uses the last file descriptor passed to the application. See section "the assuan_sendfd function" in *the Libassuan manual*, on how to do descriptor passing.

The `--armor` option may be used to advice the server that the input data is in PEM format, `--base64` advices that a raw base-64 encoding is used, `--binary` advices of raw binary input (BER). If none of these options is used, the server tries to figure out the used encoding, but this may not always be correct.

> OUTPUT FD[=*n*] [--armor|--base64]

Set the file descriptor to be used for the output (i.e. the encrypted message). Obviously the pipe must be open at that point, the server establishes its own end. If the server returns an error he client should consider this session failed.

The option armor encodes the output in PEM format, the `--base64` option applies just a base 64 encoding. No option creates binary output (BER).

The actual encryption is done using the command

> ENCRYPT

It takes the plaintext from the `INPUT` command, writes to the ciphertext to the file descriptor set with the `OUTPUT` command, take the recipients from all the recipients set so far. If this command fails the clients should try to delete all output currently done or otherwise mark it as invalid. GPGSM does ensure that there will not be any security problem with leftover data on the output in this case.

This command should in general not fail, as all necessary checks have been done while setting the recipients. The input and output pipes are closed.

5.6.2 Decrypting a message

Input and output FDs are set the same way as in encryption, but `INPUT` refers to the ciphertext and output to the plaintext. There is no need to set recipients. GPGSM automatically strips any S/MIME headers from the input, so it is valid to pass an entire MIME part to the INPUT pipe.

The encryption is done by using the command

    DECRYPT

It performs the decrypt operation after doing some check on the internal state. (e.g. that all needed data has been set). Because it utilizes the GPG-Agent for the session key decryption, there is no need to ask the client for a protecting passphrase - GpgAgent takes care of this by requesting this from the user.

5.6.3 Signing a Message

Signing is usually done with these commands:

    INPUT FD[=n] [--armor|--base64|--binary]

This tells GPGSM to read the data to sign from file descriptor n.

    OUTPUT FD[=m] [--armor|--base64]

Write the output to file descriptor m. If a detached signature is requested, only the signature is written.

    SIGN [--detached]

Sign the data set with the INPUT command and write it to the sink set by OUTPUT. With --detached, a detached signature is created (surprise).

The key used for signing is the default one or the one specified in the configuration file. To get finer control over the keys, it is possible to use the command

    SIGNER userID

to the signer's key. userID should be the internal representation of the key; the server may accept any other way of specification. If this is a valid and trusted recipient the server does respond with OK, otherwise the return is an ERR with the reason why the key cannot be used, the signature will then not be created using this key. If the policy is not to sign at all if not all keys are valid, the client has to take care of this. All SIGNER commands are cumulative until a RESET is done. Note that a SIGN does not reset this list of signers which is in contrats to the RECIPIENT command.

5.6.4 Verifying a Message

To verify a mesage the command:

    VERIFY

is used. It does a verify operation on the message send to the input FD. The result is written out using status lines. If an output FD was given, the signed text will be written to that. If the signature is a detached one, the server will inquire about the signed material and the client must provide it.

5.6.5 Generating a Key

This is used to generate a new keypair, store the secret part in the PSE and the public key in the key database. We will probably add optional commands to allow the client to select whether a hardware token is used to store the key. Configuration options to GPGSM can be used to restrict the use of this command.

    GENKEY

GPGSM checks whether this command is allowed and then does an INQUIRY to get the key parameters, the client should then send the key parameters in the native format:

```
S: INQUIRE KEY_PARAM native
C: D foo:fgfgfg
C: D bar
C: END
```

Please note that the server may send Status info lines while reading the data lines from the client. After this the key generation takes place and the server eventually does send an ERR or OK response. Status lines may be issued as a progress indicator.

5.6.6 List available keys

To list the keys in the internal database or using an external key provider, the command:

> LISTKEYS *pattern*

is used. To allow multiple patterns (which are ORed during the search) quoting is required: Spaces are to be translated into "+" or into "%20"; in turn this requires that the usual escape quoting rules are done.

> LISTSECRETKEYS *pattern*

Lists only the keys where a secret key is available.

The list commands commands are affected by the option

> OPTION list-mode=*mode*

where mode may be:

0   Use default (which is usually the same as 1).

1   List only the internal keys.

2   List only the external keys.

3   List internal and external keys.

Note that options are valid for the entire session.

5.6.7 Export certificates

To export certificate from the internal key database the command:

> EXPORT [--data [--armor] [--base64]] [--] *pattern*

is used. To allow multiple patterns (which are ORed) quoting is required: Spaces are to be translated into "+" or into "%20"; in turn this requires that the usual escape quoting rules are done.

If the '--data' option has not been given, the format of the output depends on what was set with the OUTPUT command. When using PEM encoding a few informational lines are prepended.

If the '--data' has been given, a target set via OUTPUT is ignored and the data is returned inline using standard D-lines. This avoids the need for an extra file descriptor. In this case the options '--armor' and '--base64' may be used in the same way as with the OUTPUT command.

5.6.8 Import certificates

To import certificates into the internal key database, the command

```
IMPORT [--re-import]
```

is used. The data is expected on the file descriptor set with the INPUT command. Certain checks are performed on the certificate. Note that the code will also handle PKCS#12 files and import private keys; a helper program is used for that.

With the option '--re-import' the input data is expected to a be a linefeed separated list of fingerprints. The command will re-import the corresponding certificates; that is they are made permanent by removing their ephemeral flag.

5.6.9 Delete certificates

To delete a certificate the command

```
DELKEYS pattern
```

is used. To allow multiple patterns (which are ORed) quoting is required: Spaces are to be translated into "+" or into "%20"; in turn this requires that the usual escape quoting rules are done.

The certificates must be specified unambiguously otherwise an error is returned.

5.6.10 Retrieve an audit log.

This command is used to retrieve an audit log.

```
GETAUDITLOG [--data] [--html]
```

If '--data' is used, the audit log is send using D-lines instead of being sent to the file descriptor given by an OUTPUT command. If '--html' is used, the output is formated as an XHTML block. This is designed to be incorporated into a HTML document.

5.6.11 Return information about the process

This is a multipurpose function to return a variety of information.

```
GETINFO what
```

The value of *what* specifies the kind of information returned:

version   Return the version of the program.

pid   Return the process id of the process.

agent-check
              Return OK if the agent is running.

cmd_has_option *cmd opt*
              Return OK if the command *cmd* implements the option *opt*. The leading two dashes usually used with *opt* shall not be given.

offline   Return OK if the connection is in offline mode. This may be either due to a OPTION offline=1 or due to gpgsm being started with option '--disable-dirmngr'.

5.6.12 Session options.

The standard Assuan option handler supports these options.

    OPTION name[=value]

These *names* are recognized:

putenv   Change the session's environment to be passed via gpg-agent to Pinentry. *value*
           is a string of the form `<KEY>[=[<STRING>]]`. If only `<KEY>` is given the envi-
           ronment variable `<KEY>` is removed from the session environment, if `<KEY>=` is
           given that environment variable is set to the empty string, and if `<STRING>` is
           given it is set to that string.

display   Set the session environment variable `DISPLAY` is set to *value*.

ttyname   Set the session environment variable `GPG_TTY` is set to *value*.

ttytype   Set the session environment variable `TERM` is set to *value*.

lc-ctype   Set the session environment variable `LC_CTYPE` is set to *value*.

lc-messages
           Set the session environment variable `LC_MESSAGES` is set to *value*.

xauthority
           Set the session environment variable `XAUTHORITY` is set to *value*.

pinentry-user-data
           Set the session environment variable `PINENTRY_USER_DATA` is set to *value*.

include-certs
           This option overrides the command line option '`--include-certs`'. A *value* of -
           2 includes all certificates except for the root certificate, -1 includes all certicates,
           0 does not include any certicates, 1 includes only the signers certicate and all
           other positive values include up to *value* certificates starting with the signer
           cert.

list-mode
           See [gpgsm-cmd listkeys], page 97.

list-to-output
           If *value* is true the output of the list commands (see [gpgsm-cmd listkeys],
           page 97) is written to the file descriptor set with the last OUTPUT command.
           If *value* is false the output is written via data lines; this is the default.

with-validation
           If *value* is true for each listed certificate the validation status is printed. This
           may result in the download of a CRL or the user being asked about the trust-
           worthiness of a root certificate. The default is given by a command line option
           (see [gpgsm-option –with-validation], page 87).

with-secret
           If *value* is true certificates with a corresponding private key are marked by the
           list commands.

`validation-model`

> This option overrides the command line option 'validation-model' for the session. (see [gpgsm-option –validation-model], page 86.)

`with-key-data`

> This option globally enables the command line option '--with-key-data'. (see [gpgsm-option –with-key-data], page 87.)

`enable-audit-log`

> If *value* is true data to write an audit log is gathered. (see [gpgsm-cmd getauditlog], page 98.)

`allow-pinentry-notify`

> If this option is used notifications about the launch of a Pinentry are passed back to the client.

`with-ephemeral-keys`

> If *value* is true ephemeral certificates are included in the output of the list commands.

`no-encrypt-to`

> If this option is used all keys set by the command line option '--encrypt-to' are ignored.

`offline`   If *value* is true or *value* is not given all network access is disabled for this session. This is the same as the command line option '--disable-dirmngr'.

6 Invoking the SCDAEMON

The `scdaemon` is a daemon to manage smartcards. It is usually invoked by `gpg-agent` and in general not used directly.

See [Option Index], page 167, for an index to `scdaemon`'s commands and options.

6.1 Commands

Commands are not distinguished from options except for the fact that only one command is allowed.

`--version`

> Print the program version and licensing information. Not that you can abbreviate this command.

`--help, -h`

> Print a usage message summarizing the most useful command-line options. Not that you can abbreviate this command.

`--dump-options`

> Print a list of all available options and commands. Not that you can abbreviate this command.

`--server` Run in server mode and wait for commands on the `stdin`. This is default mode is to create a socket and listen for commands there.

`--multi-server`

> Run in server mode and wait for commands on the `stdin` as well as on an additional Unix Domain socket. The server command `GETINFO` may be used to get the name of that extra socket.

`--daemon` Run the program in the background. This option is required to prevent it from being accidentally running in the background.

6.2 Option Summary

`--options file`

> Reads configuration from *file* instead of from the default per-user configuration file. The default configuration file is named '`scdaemon.conf`' and expected in the '`.gnupg`' directory directly below the home directory of the user.

`--homedir dir`

> Set the name of the home directory to *dir*. If this option is not used, the home directory defaults to '`~/.gnupg`'. It is only recognized when given on the command line. It also overrides any home directory stated through the environment variable `GNUPGHOME` or (on Windows systems) by means of the Registry entry *HKCU\Software\GNU\GnuPG:HomeDir*.
>
> On Windows systems it is possible to install GnuPG as a portable application. In this case only this command line option is considered, all other ways to set a home directory are ignored.

To install GnuPG as a portable application under Windows, create an empty file name 'gpgconf.ctl' in the same directory as the tool 'gpgconf.exe'. The root of the installation is than that directory; or, if 'gpgconf.exe' has been installed directly below a directory named 'bin', its parent directory. You also need to make sure that the following directories exist and are writable: 'ROOT/home' for the GnuPG home and 'ROOT/usr/local/var/cache/gnupg' for internal cache files.

`-v`

`--verbose`

Outputs additional information while running. You can increase the verbosity by giving several verbose commands to gpgsm, such as '-vv'.

`--debug-level` *level*

Select the debug level for investigating problems. *level* may be a numeric value or a keyword:

`none`   No debugging at all. A value of less than 1 may be used instead of the keyword.

`basic`   Some basic debug messages. A value between 1 and 2 may be used instead of the keyword.

`advanced` More verbose debug messages. A value between 3 and 5 may be used instead of the keyword.

`expert`   Even more detailed messages. A value between 6 and 8 may be used instead of the keyword.

`guru`   All of the debug messages you can get. A value greater than 8 may be used instead of the keyword. The creation of hash tracing files is only enabled if the keyword is used.

How these messages are mapped to the actual debugging flags is not specified and may change with newer releases of this program. They are however carefully selected to best aid in debugging.

> **Note:** All debugging options are subject to change and thus should not be used by any application program. As the name says, they are only used as helpers to debug problems.

`--debug` *flags*

This option is only useful for debugging and the behaviour may change at any time without notice. FLAGS are bit encoded and may be given in usual C-Syntax. The currently defined bits are:

0 (1)   command I/O

1 (2)   values of big number integers

2 (4)   low level crypto operations

5 (32)   memory allocation

6 (64)   caching

7 (128) show memory statistics.

9 (512) write hashed data to files named `dbgmd-000*`

10 (1024) trace Assuan protocol. See also option '`--debug-assuan-log-cats`'.█

11 (2048) trace APDU I/O to the card. This may reveal sensitive data.

12 (4096) trace some card reader related function calls.

`--debug-all`

Same as `--debug=0xffffffff`

`--debug-wait n`

When running in server mode, wait *n* seconds before entering the actual processing loop and print the pid. This gives time to attach a debugger.

`--debug-ccid-driver`

Enable debug output from the included CCID driver for smartcards. Using this option twice will also enable some tracing of the T=1 protocol. Note that this option may reveal sensitive data.

`--debug-disable-ticker`

This option disables all ticker functions like checking for card insertions.

`--debug-allow-core-dump`

For security reasons we won't create a core dump when the process aborts. For debugging purposes it is sometimes better to allow core dump. This options enables it and also changes the working directory to '`/tmp`' when running in '`--server`' mode.

`--debug-log-tid`

This option appends a thread ID to the PID in the log output.

`--debug-assuan-log-cats cats`

Changes the active Libassuan logging categories to *cats*. The value for *cats* is an unsigned integer given in usual C-Syntax. A value of of 0 switches to a default category. If this option is not used the categories are taken from the environment variable '`ASSUAN_DEBUG`'. Note that this option has only an effect if the Assuan debug flag has also been with the option '`--debug`'. For a list of categories see the Libassuan manual.

`--no-detach`

Don't detach the process from the console. This is mainly useful for debugging.

`--log-file file`

Append all logging output to *file*. This is very helpful in seeing what the agent actually does.

`--pcsc-driver library`

Use *library* to access the smartcard reader. The current default is '`libpcsclite.so`'. Instead of using this option you might also want to install a symbolic link to the default file name (e.g. from '`libpcsclite.so.1`').

`--ctapi-driver` *library*

> Use *library* to access the smartcard reader. The current default is `libtowitoko.so`. Note that the use of this interface is deprecated; it may be removed in future releases.

`--disable-ccid`

> Disable the integrated support for CCID compliant readers. This allows to fall back to one of the other drivers even if the internal CCID driver can handle the reader. Note, that CCID support is only available if libusb was available at build time.

`--reader-port` *number_or_string*

> This option may be used to specify the port of the card terminal. A value of 0 refers to the first serial device; add 32768 to access USB devices. The default is 32768 (first USB device). PC/SC or CCID readers might need a string here; run the program in verbose mode to get a list of available readers. The default is then the first reader found.
>
> To get a list of available CCID readers you may use this command:

```
echo scd getinfo reader_list \
   | gpg-connect-agent --decode | awk '/^D/ {print $2}'
```

`--card-timeout` *n*

> If *n* is not 0 and no client is actively using the card, the card will be powered down after *n* seconds. Powering down the card avoids a potential risk of damaging a card when used with certain cheap readers. This also allows non Scdaemon aware applications to access the card. The disadvantage of using a card timeout is that accessing the card takes longer and that the user needs to enter the PIN again after the next power up.
>
> Note that with the current version of Scdaemon the card is powered down immediately at the next timer tick for any value of *n* other than 0.

`--enable-pinpad-varlen`

> Please specify this option when the card reader supports variable length input for pinpad (default is no). For known readers (listed in ccid-driver.c and apdu.c), this option is not needed. Note that if your card reader doesn't supports variable length input but you want to use it, you need to specify your pinpad request on your card.

`--disable-pinpad`

> Even if a card reader features a pinpad, do not try to use it.

`--deny-admin`

> This option disables the use of admin class commands for card applications where this is supported. Currently we support it for the OpenPGP card. This commands is useful to inhibit accidental access to admin class command which could ultimately lock the card through wrong PIN numbers. Note that GnuPG versions older than 2.0.11 featured an '`--allow-admin`' command which was required to use such admin commands. This option has no more effect today because the default is now to allow admin commands.

`--disable-application` *name*

> This option disables the use of the card application named *name*. This is mainly useful for debugging or if a application with lower priority should be used by default.

All the long options may also be given in the configuration file after stripping off the two leading dashes.

6.3 Description of card applications

`scdaemon` supports the card applications as described below.

6.3.1 The OpenPGP card application "openpgp"

This application is currently only used by **gpg** but may in future also be useful with **gpgsm**. Version 1 and version 2 of the card is supported.

The specifications for these cards are available at
`http://g10code.com/docs/openpgp-card-1.0.pdf` and
`http://g10code.com/docs/openpgp-card-2.0.pdf`.

6.3.2 The Telesec NetKey card "nks"

This is the main application of the Telesec cards as available in Germany. It is a superset of the German DINSIG card. The card is used by **gpgsm**.

6.3.3 The DINSIG card application "dinsig"

This is an application as described in the German draft standard *DIN V 66291-1*. It is intended to be used by cards supporting the German signature law and its bylaws (SigG and SigV).

6.3.4 The PKCS#15 card application "p15"

This is common framework for smart card applications. It is used by **gpgsm**.

6.3.5 The Geldkarte card application "geldkarte"

This is a simple application to display information of a German Geldkarte. The Geldkarte is a small amount debit card application which comes with almost all German banking cards.

6.3.6 The SmartCard-HSM card application "sc-hsm"

This application adds read/only support for keys and certificates stored on a SmartCard-HSM.

To generate keys and store certificates you may use OpenSC or the tools from OpenSCDP.

The SmartCard-HSM cards requires a card reader that supports Extended Length APDUs.

6.3.7 The Undefined card application "undefined"

This is a stub application to allow the use of the APDU command even if no supported application is found on the card. This application is not used automatically but must be explicitly requested using the SERIALNO command.

6.4 Configuration files

There are a few configuration files to control certain aspects of scdaemons's operation. Unless noted, they are expected in the current home directory (see [option –homedir], page 4).

'scdaemon.conf'

> This is the standard configuration file read by scdaemon on startup. It may contain any valid long option; the leading two dashes may not be entered and the option may not be abbreviated. This default name may be changed on the command line (see [option –options], page 4).

'scd-event'

> If this file is present and executable, it will be called on veyer card reader's status changed. An example of this script is provided with the distribution

'reader_n.status'

> This file is created by sdaemon to let other applications now about reader status changes. Its use is now deprecated in favor of 'scd-event'.

6.5 Examples

```
$ scdaemon --server -v
```

6.6 Scdaemon's Assuan Protocol

The SC-Daemon should be started by the system to provide access to external tokens. Using Smartcards on a multi-user system does not make much sense expect for system services, but in this case no regular user accounts are hosted on the machine.

A client connects to the SC-Daemon by connecting to the socket named '/usr/local/var/run/gnupg/scdaemon/socket', configuration information is read from /usr/local/etc/gnupg/scdaemon.conf

Each connection acts as one session, SC-Daemon takes care of synchronizing access to a token between sessions.

6.6.1 Return the serial number

This command should be used to check for the presence of a card. It is special in that it can be used to reset the card. Most other commands will return an error when a card change has been detected and the use of this function is therefore required.

Background: We want to keep the client clear of handling card changes between operations; i.e. the client can assume that all operations are done on the same card unless he call this function.

```
SERIALNO
```

Return the serial number of the card using a status response like:

```
S SERIALNO D27600000000000000000000 0
```

The trailing 0 should be ignored for now, it is reserved for a future extension. The serial number is the hex encoded value identified by the 0x5A tag in the GDO file (FIX=0x2F02).

6.6.2 Read all useful information from the card

    LEARN [--force]

Learn all useful information of the currently inserted card. When used without the force options, the command might do an INQUIRE like this:

        INQUIRE KNOWNCARDP <hexstring_with_serialNumber> <timestamp>

The client should just send an END if the processing should go on or a CANCEL to force the function to terminate with a cancel error message. The response of this command is a list of status lines formatted as this:

        S KEYPAIRINFO *hexstring_with_keygrip* *hexstring_with_id*

If there is no certificate yet stored on the card a single "X" is returned in *hexstring_with_keygrip*.

6.6.3 Return a certificate

    READCERT *hexified_certid|keyid*

This function is used to read a certificate identified by *hexified_certid* from the card. With OpenPGP cards the keyid OpenPGP.3 may be used to rad the certificate of version 2 cards.

6.6.4 Return a public key

    READKEY *hexified_certid*

Return the public key for the given cert or key ID as an standard S-Expression.

6.6.5 Signing data with a Smartcard

To sign some data the caller should use the command

    SETDATA *hexstring*

to tell scdaemon about the data to be signed. The data must be given in hex notation. The actual signing is done using the command

    PKSIGN *keyid*

where *keyid* is the hexified ID of the key to be used. The key id may have been retrieved using the command LEARN. If another hash algorithm than SHA-1 is used, that algorithm may be given like:

    PKSIGN --hash=*algoname* *keyid*

With *algoname* are one of sha1, rmd160 or md5.

6.6.6 Decrypting data with a Smartcard

To decrypt some data the caller should use the command

    SETDATA *hexstring*

to tell scdaemon about the data to be decrypted. The data must be given in hex notation. The actual decryption is then done using the command

    PKDECRYPT *keyid*

where *keyid* is the hexified ID of the key to be used.

If the card is ware of the apdding format a status line with padding information is send before the plaintext data. The key for this status line is `PADDING` with the only defined value being 0 and meaning padding has been removed.

6.6.7 Read an attribute's value.

TO BE WRITTEN.

6.6.8 Update an attribute's value.

TO BE WRITTEN.

6.6.9 Write a key to a card.

> `WRITEKEY [--force] keyid`

This command is used to store a secret key on a smartcard. The allowed keyids depend on the currently selected smartcard application. The actual keydata is requested using the inquiry `KEYDATA` and need to be provided without any protection. With '`--force`' set an existing key under this *keyid* will get overwritten. The key data is expected to be the usual canonical encoded S-expression.

A PIN will be requested in most cases. This however depends on the actual card application.

6.6.10 Generate a new key on-card.

TO BE WRITTEN.

6.6.11 Return random bytes generate on-card.

TO BE WRITTEN.

6.6.12 Change PINs.

> `PASSWD [--reset] [--nullpin] chvno`

Change the PIN or reset the retry counter of the card holder verification vector number *chvno*. The option '`--nullpin`' is used to initialize the PIN of TCOS cards (6 byte NullPIN only).

6.6.13 Perform a VERIFY operation.

> `CHECKPIN idstr`

Perform a VERIFY operation without doing anything else. This may be used to initialize a the PIN cache earlier to long lasting operations. Its use is highly application dependent:

OpenPGP

> Perform a simple verify operation for CHV1 and CHV2, so that further operations won't ask for CHV2 and it is possible to do a cheap check on the PIN: If there is something wrong with the PIN entry system, only the regular CHV will get blocked and not the dangerous CHV3. *idstr* is the usual card's serial number in hex notation; an optional fingerprint part will get ignored.
>
> There is however a special mode if *idstr* is suffixed with the literal string `[CHV3]`: In this case the Admin PIN is checked if and only if the retry counter is still at 3.

6.6.14 Perform a RESTART operation.

```
RESTART
```

Restart the current connection; this is a kind of warm reset. It deletes the context used by this connection but does not actually reset the card.

This is used by gpg-agent to reuse a primary pipe connection and may be used by clients to backup from a conflict in the serial command; i.e. to select another application.

6.6.15 Send a verbatim APDU to the card.

```
APDU [--atr] [--more] [--exlen[=n]] [hexstring]
```

Send an APDU to the current reader. This command bypasses the high level functions and sends the data directly to the card. *hexstring* is expected to be a proper APDU. If *hexstring* is not given no commands are send to the card; However the command will implicitly check whether the card is ready for use.

Using the option `--atr` returns the ATR of the card as a status message before any data like this:

```
S CARD-ATR 3BFA1300FF813180450031C173C00100009000B1
```

Using the option `--more` handles the card status word MORE_DATA (61xx) and concatenate all responses to one block.

Using the option `--exlen` the returned APDU may use extended length up to N bytes. If N is not given a default value is used (currently 4096).

7 How to Specify a User Id

There are different ways to specify a user ID to GnuPG. Some of them are only valid for gpg others are only good for gpgsm. Here is the entire list of ways to specify a key:

- By key Id. This format is deduced from the length of the string and its content or 0x prefix. The key Id of an X.509 certificate are the low 64 bits of its SHA-1 fingerprint. The use of key Ids is just a shortcut, for all automated processing the fingerprint should be used.

  When using gpg an exclamation mark (!) may be appended to force using the specified primary or secondary key and not to try and calculate which primary or secondary key to use.

  The last four lines of the example give the key ID in their long form as internally used by the OpenPGP protocol. You can see the long key ID using the option '--with-colons'.

```
234567C4
0F34E556E
01347A56A
0xAB123456

234AABBCC34567C4
0F323456784E56EAB
01AB3FED1347A5612
0x234AABBCC34567C4
```

- By fingerprint. This format is deduced from the length of the string and its content or the 0x prefix. Note, that only the 20 byte version fingerprint is available with gpgsm (i.e. the SHA-1 hash of the certificate).

  When using gpg an exclamation mark (!) may be appended to force using the specified primary or secondary key and not to try and calculate which primary or secondary key to use.

  The best way to specify a key Id is by using the fingerprint. This avoids any ambiguities in case that there are duplicated key IDs.

```
1234343434343434C434343434343434
12343434343434343C343434343434343734349A3434
0E1234343434343434343434EAB3484343434343434
0xE1234343434343434343434EAB3484343434343434
```

gpgsm also accepts colons between each pair of hexadecimal digits because this is the de-facto standard on how to present X.509 fingerprints. gpg also allows the use of the space separated SHA-1 fingerprint as printed by the key listing commands.

- By exact match on OpenPGP user ID. This is denoted by a leading equal sign. It does not make sense for X.509 certificates.

```
=Heinrich Heine <heinrichh@uni-duesseldorf.de>
```

- By exact match on an email address. This is indicated by enclosing the email address in the usual way with left and right angles.

```
<heinrichh@uni-duesseldorf.de>
```

- By partial match on an email address. This is indicated by prefixing the search string with an @. This uses a substring search but considers only the mail address (i.e. inside the angle brackets).

```
@heinrichh
```

- By exact match on the subject's DN. This is indicated by a leading slash, directly followed by the RFC-2253 encoded DN of the subject. Note that you can't use the string printed by "gpgsm –list-keys" because that one as been reordered and modified for better readability; use –with-colons to print the raw (but standard escaped) RFC-2253 string

```
/CN=Heinrich Heine,O=Poets,L=Paris,C=FR
```

- By exact match on the issuer's DN. This is indicated by a leading hash mark, directly followed by a slash and then directly followed by the rfc2253 encoded DN of the issuer. This should return the Root cert of the issuer. See note above.

```
#/CN=Root Cert,O=Poets,L=Paris,C=FR
```

- By exact match on serial number and issuer's DN. This is indicated by a hash mark, followed by the hexadecimal representation of the serial number, then followed by a slash and the RFC-2253 encoded DN of the issuer. See note above.

```
#4F03/CN=Root Cert,O=Poets,L=Paris,C=FR
```

- By keygrip This is indicated by an ampersand followed by the 40 hex digits of a keygrip. gpgsm prints the keygrip when using the command '--dump-cert'. It does not yet work for OpenPGP keys.

```
&D75F22C3F86E355877348498CDC92BD21010A480
```

- By substring match. This is the default mode but applications may want to explicitly indicate this by putting the asterisk in front. Match is not case sensitive.

```
Heine
*Heine
```

- . and + prefixes These prefixes are reserved for looking up mails anchored at the end and for a word search mode. They are not yet implemented and using them is undefined.

Please note that we have reused the hash mark identifier which was used in old GnuPG versions to indicate the so called local-id. It is not anymore used and there should be no conflict when used with X.509 stuff.

Using the RFC-2253 format of DNs has the drawback that it is not possible to map them back to the original encoding, however we don't have to do this because our key database stores this encoding as meta data.

8 Helper Tools

GnuPG comes with a couple of smaller tools:

8.1 Read logs from a socket

Most of the main utilities are able to write their log files to a Unix Domain socket if configured that way. `watchgnupg` is a simple listener for such a socket. It ameliorates the output with a time stamp and makes sure that long lines are not interspersed with log output from other utilities. This tool is not available for Windows.

`watchgnupg` is commonly invoked as

        watchgnupg --force ~/.gnupg/S.log

This starts it on the current terminal for listening on the socket '`~/.gnupg/S.log`'.

`watchgnupg` understands these options:

`--force`   Delete an already existing socket file.

`--tcp n`   Instead of reading from a local socket, listen for connects on TCP port n.

`--verbose`
        Enable extra informational output.

`--version`
        Print version of the program and exit.

`--help`   Display a brief help page and exit.

Examples

        $ watchgnupg --force /home/foo/.gnupg/S.log

This waits for connections on the local socket '`/home/foo/.gnupg/S.log`' and shows all log entries. To make this work the option '`log-file`' needs to be used with all modules which logs are to be shown. The value for that option must be given with a special prefix (e.g. in the conf file):

        log-file socket:///home/foo/.gnupg/S.log

For debugging purposes it is also possible to do remote logging. Take care if you use this feature because the information is send in the clear over the network. Use this syntax in the conf files:

        log-file tcp://192.168.1.1:4711

You may use any port and not just 4711 as shown above; only IP addresses are supported (v4 and v6) and no host names. You need to start `watchgnupg` with the '`tcp`' option. Note that under Windows the registry entry *HKCU\Software\GNU\GnuPG:DefaultLogFile* can be used to change the default log output from **stderr** to whatever is given by that entry. However the only useful entry is a TCP name for remote debugging.

8.2 Verify OpenPGP signatures

gpgv2 is an OpenPGP signature verification tool.

This program is actually a stripped-down version of **gpg** which is only able to check signatures. It is somewhat smaller than the fully-blown **gpg** and uses a different (and simpler) way to check that the public keys used to make the signature are valid. There are no configuration files and only a few options are implemented.

gpgv2 assumes that all keys in the keyring are trustworthy. That does also mean that it does not check for expired or revoked keys.

By default a keyring named '**trustedkeys.kbx**' is used; if that does not exist a keyring named '**trustedkeys.gpg**' is used. The default keyring is assumed to be in the home directory of GnuPG, either the default home directory or the one set by an option or an environment variable. The option **--keyring** may be used to specify a different keyring or even multiple keyrings.

gpgv2 recognizes these options:

--verbose
-v   Gives more information during processing. If used twice, the input data is listed in detail.

--quiet
-q   Try to be as quiet as possible.

--keyring *file*
          Add *file* to the list of keyrings. If *file* begins with a tilde and a slash, these are replaced by the HOME directory. If the filename does not contain a slash, it is assumed to be in the home-directory ("~/.gnupg" if –homedir is not used).

--status-fd *n*
          Write special status strings to the file descriptor *n*. See the file DETAILS in the documentation for a listing of them.

--logger-fd n
          Write log output to file descriptor **n** and not to stderr.

--ignore-time-conflict
          GnuPG normally checks that the timestamps associated with keys and signatures have plausible values. However, sometimes a signature seems to be older than the key due to clock problems. This option turns these checks into warnings.

--homedir *dir*
          Set the name of the home directory to *dir*. If this option is not used, the home directory defaults to '~/.gnupg'. It is only recognized when given on the command line. It also overrides any home directory stated through the environment variable **GNUPGHOME** or (on Windows systems) by means of the Registry entry *HKCU\Software\GNU\GnuPG:HomeDir*.

          On Windows systems it is possible to install GnuPG as a portable application. In this case only this command line option is considered, all other ways to set a home directory are ignored.

To install GnuPG as a portable application under Windows, create an empty file name 'gpgconf.ctl' in the same directory as the tool 'gpgconf.exe'. The root of the installation is than that directory; or, if 'gpgconf.exe' has been installed directly below a directory named 'bin', its parent directory. You also need to make sure that the following directories exist and are writable: 'ROOT/home' for the GnuPG home and 'ROOT/usr/local/var/cache/gnupg' for internal cache files.

The program returns 0 if everything is fine, 1 if at least one signature was bad, and other error codes for fatal errors.

8.2.1 Examples

gpgv2 pgpfile
gpgv2 sigfile [datafile]
> Verify the signature of the file. The second form is used for detached signatures, where sigfile is the detached signature (either ASCII-armored or binary) and datafile contains the signed data; if datafile is "-" the signed data is expected on stdin; if datafile is not given the name of the file holding the signed data is constructed by cutting off the extension (".asc", ".sig" or ".sign") from sigfile.

8.2.2 Environment

HOME   Used to locate the default home directory.

GNUPGHOME
> If set directory used instead of "~/.gnupg".

8.2.3 FILES

~/.gnupg/trustedkeys.gpg
> The default keyring with the allowed keys.

gpg2(1)

8.3 Create .gnupg home directories.

If GnuPG is installed on a system with existing user accounts, it is sometimes required to populate the GnuPG home directory with existing files. Especially a 'trustlist.txt' and a keybox with some initial certificates are often desired. This scripts help to do this by copying all files from '/etc/skel/.gnupg' to the home directories of the accounts given on the command line. It takes care not to overwrite existing GnuPG home directories.

addgnupghome is invoked by root as:

        addgnupghome account1 account2 ... accountn

8.4 Modify .gnupg home directories.

The `gpgconf` is a utility to automatically and reasonable safely query and modify configuration files in the '.gnupg' home directory. It is designed not to be invoked manually by the user, but automatically by graphical user interfaces (GUI).[1]

`gpgconf` provides access to the configuration of one or more components of the GnuPG system. These components correspond more or less to the programs that exist in the GnuPG framework, like GnuPG, GPGSM, DirMngr, etc. But this is not a strict one-to-one relationship. Not all configuration options are available through `gpgconf`. `gpgconf` provides a generic and abstract method to access the most important configuration options that can feasibly be controlled via such a mechanism.

`gpgconf` can be used to gather and change the options available in each component, and can also provide their default values. `gpgconf` will give detailed type information that can be used to restrict the user's input without making an attempt to commit the changes.

`gpgconf` provides the backend of a configuration editor. The configuration editor would usually be a graphical user interface program, that allows to display the current options, their default values, and allows the user to make changes to the options. These changes can then be made active with `gpgconf` again. Such a program that uses `gpgconf` in this way will be called GUI throughout this section.

8.4.1 Invoking gpgconf

One of the following commands must be given:

`--list-components`

> List all components. This is the default command used if none is specified.

`--check-programs`

> List all available backend programs and test whether they are runnable.

`--list-options` *component*

> List all options of the component *component*.

`--change-options` *component*

> Change the options of the component *component*.

`--check-options` *component*

> Check the options for the component *component*.

`--apply-defaults`

> Update all configuration files with values taken from the global configuration file (usually '/etc/gnupg/gpgconf.conf').

`--list-dirs`

> Lists the directories used by `gpgconf`. One directory is listed per line, and each line consists of a colon-separated list where the first field names the directory type (for example `sysconfdir`) and the second field contains the percent-escaped directory. Although they are not directories, the socket file names used

---

[1] Please note that currently no locking is done, so concurrent access should be avoided. There are some precautions to avoid corruption with concurrent usage, but results may be inconsistent and some changes may get lost. The stateless design makes it difficult to provide more guarantees.

by `gpg-agent` and `dirmngr` are printed as well. Note that the socket file names and the `homedir` lines are the default names and they may be overridden by command line switches.

`--list-config [filename]`

List the global configuration file in a colon separated format. If *filename* is given, check that file instead.

`--check-config [filename]`

Run a syntax check on the global configuration file. If *filename* is given, check that file instead.

`--reload [component]`

Reload all or the given component. This is basically the same as sending a SIGHUP to the component. Components which don't support reloading are ignored.

`--launch [component]`

If the *component* is not already running, start it. `component` must be a daemon. This is in general not required because the system starts these daemons as needed. However, external software making direct use of `gpg-agent` or `dirmngr` may use this command to ensure that they are started.

`--kill [component]`

Kill the given component. Components which support killing are gpg-agent and scdaemon. Components which don't support reloading are ignored. Note that as of now reload and kill have the same effect for scdaemon.

The following options may be used:

`-o file`
`--output file`

Write output to *file*. Default is to write to stdout.

`-v`
`--verbose`

Outputs additional information while running. Specifically, this extends numerical field values by human-readable descriptions.

`-q`
`--quiet`   Try to be as quiet as possible.

`-n`
`--dry-run`

Do not actually change anything. This is currently only implemented for `--change-options` and can be used for testing purposes.

`-r`
`--runtime`

Only used together with `--change-options`. If one of the modified options can be changed in a running daemon process, signal the running daemon to ask it to reparse its configuration file after changing.

This means that the changes will take effect at run-time, as far as this is possible. Otherwise, they will take effect at the next start of the respective backend programs.

8.4.2 Format conventions

Some lines in the output of `gpgconf` contain a list of colon-separated fields. The following conventions apply:

- The GUI program is required to strip off trailing newline and/or carriage return characters from the output.

- `gpgconf` will never leave out fields. If a certain version provides a certain field, this field will always be present in all `gpgconf` versions from that time on.

- Future versions of `gpgconf` might append fields to the list. New fields will always be separated from the previously last field by a colon separator. The GUI should be prepared to parse the last field it knows about up until a colon or end of line.

- Not all fields are defined under all conditions. You are required to ignore the content of undefined fields.

There are several standard types for the content of a field:

verbatim   Some fields contain strings that are not escaped in any way. Such fields are described to be used *verbatim*. These fields will never contain a colon character (for obvious reasons). No de-escaping or other formatting is required to use the field content. This is for easy parsing of the output, when it is known that the content can never contain any special characters.

percent-escaped
Some fields contain strings that are described to be *percent-escaped*. Such strings need to be de-escaped before their content can be presented to the user. A percent-escaped string is de-escaped by replacing all occurrences of `%XY` by the byte that has the hexadecimal value `XY`. `X` and `Y` are from the set `0-9a-f`.

localised   Some fields contain strings that are described to be *localised*. Such strings are translated to the active language and formatted in the active character set.

unsigned number
Some fields contain an *unsigned number*. This number will always fit into a 32-bit unsigned integer variable. The number may be followed by a space, followed by a human readable description of that value (if the verbose option is used). You should ignore everything in the field that follows the number.

signed number
Some fields contain a *signed number*. This number will always fit into a 32-bit signed integer variable. The number may be followed by a space, followed by a human readable description of that value (if the verbose option is used). You should ignore everything in the field that follows the number.

boolean value
Some fields contain a *boolean value*. This is a number with either the value 0 or 1. The number may be followed by a space, followed by a human readable description of that value (if the verbose option is used). You should ignore

everything in the field that follows the number; checking just the first character is sufficient in this case.

option   Some fields contain an *option* argument. The format of an option argument depends on the type of the option and on some flags:

no argument

> The simplest case is that the option does not take an argument at all (*type* 0). Then the option argument is an unsigned number that specifies how often the option occurs. If the `list` flag is not set, then the only valid number is 1. Options that do not take an argument never have the `default` or `optional arg` flag set.

number   If the option takes a number argument (*alt-type* is 2 or 3), and it can only occur once (`list` flag is not set), then the option argument is either empty (only allowed if the argument is optional), or it is a number. A number is a string that begins with an optional minus character, followed by one or more digits. The number must fit into an integer variable (unsigned or signed, depending on *alt-type*).

number list

> If the option takes a number argument and it can occur more than once, then the option argument is either empty, or it is a comma-separated list of numbers as described above.

string   If the option takes a string argument (*alt-type* is 1), and it can only occur once (`list` flag is not set) then the option argument is either empty (only allowed if the argument is optional), or it starts with a double quote character (") followed by a percent-escaped string that is the argument value. Note that there is only a leading double quote character, no trailing one. The double quote character is only needed to be able to differentiate between no value and the empty string as value.

string list If the option takes a number argument and it can occur more than once, then the option argument is either empty, or it is a comma-separated list of string arguments as described above.

The active language and character set are currently determined from the locale environment of the `gpgconf` program.

8.4.3 Listing components

The command `--list-components` will list all components that can be configured with `gpgconf`. Usually, one component will correspond to one GnuPG-related program and contain the options of that programs configuration file that can be modified using `gpgconf`. However, this is not necessarily the case. A component might also be a group of selected options from several programs, or contain entirely virtual options that have a special effect rather than changing exactly one option in one configuration file.

A component is a set of configuration options that semantically belong together. Furthermore, several changes to a component can be made in an atomic way with a single operation. The GUI could for example provide a menu with one entry for each component, or a window with one tabulator sheet per component.

The command argument `--list-components` lists all available components, one per line. The format of each line is:

name:*description*:*pgmname*:

name   This field contains a name tag of the component. The name tag is used to specify the component in all communication with `gpgconf`. The name tag is to be used *verbatim*. It is thus not in any escaped format.

description

      The *string* in this field contains a human-readable description of the component. It can be displayed to the user of the GUI for informational purposes. It is *percent-escaped* and *localized*.

pgmname   The *string* in this field contains the absolute name of the program's file. It can be used to unambiguously invoke that program. It is *percent-escaped*.

Example:

```
$ gpgconf --list-components
gpg:GPG for OpenPGP:/usr/local/bin/gpg2:
gpg-agent:GPG Agent:/usr/local/bin/gpg-agent:
scdaemon:Smartcard Daemon:/usr/local/bin/scdaemon:
gpgsm:GPG for S/MIME:/usr/local/bin/gpgsm:
dirmngr:Directory Manager:/usr/local/bin/dirmngr:
```

8.4.4 Checking programs

The command `--check-programs` is similar to `--list-components` but works on backend programs and not on components. It runs each program to test whether it is installed and runnable. This also includes a syntax check of all config file options of the program.

The command argument `--check-programs` lists all available programs, one per line. The format of each line is:

name:*description*:*pgmname*:*avail*:*okay*:*cfgfile*:*line*:*error*:

name   This field contains a name tag of the program which is identical to the name of the component. The name tag is to be used *verbatim*. It is thus not in any escaped format. This field may be empty to indicate a continuation of error descriptions for the last name. The description and pgmname fields are then also empty.

description

      The *string* in this field contains a human-readable description of the component. It can be displayed to the user of the GUI for informational purposes. It is *percent-escaped* and *localized*.

pgmname   The *string* in this field contains the absolute name of the program's file. It can be used to unambiguously invoke that program. It is *percent-escaped*.

avail   The *boolean value* in this field indicates whether the program is installed and runnable.

okay   The *boolean value* in this field indicates whether the program's config file is
              syntactically okay.

cfgfile   If an error occurred in the configuration file (as indicated by a false value in
              the field `okay`), this field has the name of the failing configuration file. It is
              percent-escaped.

line   If an error occurred in the configuration file, this field has the line number of
              the failing statement in the configuration file. It is an *unsigned number*.

error   If an error occurred in the configuration file, this field has the error text of the
              failing statement in the configuration file. It is *percent-escaped* and *localized*.

In the following example the `dirmngr` is not runnable and the configuration file of `scdaemon`
is not okay.

```
$ gpgconf --check-programs
gpg:GPG for OpenPGP:/usr/local/bin/gpg2:1:1:
gpg-agent:GPG Agent:/usr/local/bin/gpg-agent:1:1:
scdaemon:Smartcard Daemon:/usr/local/bin/scdaemon:1:0:
gpgsm:GPG for S/MIME:/usr/local/bin/gpgsm:1:1:
dirmngr:Directory Manager:/usr/local/bin/dirmngr:0:0:
```

The command `--check-options` *component* will verify the configuration file in the same
manner as `--check-programs`, but only for the component *component*.

8.4.5 Listing options

Every component contains one or more options. Options may be gathered into option
groups to allow the GUI to give visual hints to the user about which options are related.

The command argument `--list-options` *component* lists all options (and the groups
they belong to) in the component *component*, one per line. *component* must be the string
in the field *name* in the output of the `--list-components` command.

There is one line for each option and each group. First come all options that are not in
any group. Then comes a line describing a group. Then come all options that belong into
each group. Then comes the next group and so on. There does not need to be any group
(and in this case the output will stop after the last non-grouped option).

The format of each line is:

`name:flags:level:description:type:alt-type:argname:default:argdef:value`

name   This field contains a name tag for the group or option. The name tag is used
              to specify the group or option in all communication with `gpgconf`. The name
              tag is to be used *verbatim*. It is thus not in any escaped format.

flags   The flags field contains an *unsigned number*. Its value is the OR-wise combina-
              tion of the following flag values:

              group (1) If this flag is set, this is a line describing a group and not an option.

              The following flag values are only defined for options (that is, if the **group** flag
              is not used).

optional arg (2)
> If this flag is set, the argument is optional. This is never set for *type* 0 (none) options.

list (4)   If this flag is set, the option can be given multiple times.

runtime (8)
> If this flag is set, the option can be changed at runtime.

default (16)
> If this flag is set, a default value is available.

default desc (32)
> If this flag is set, a (runtime) default is available. This and the **default** flag are mutually exclusive.

no arg desc (64)
> If this flag is set, and the **optional arg** flag is set, then the option has a special meaning if no argument is given.

no change (128)
> If this flag is set, gpgconf ignores requests to change the value. GUI frontends should grey out this option. Note, that manual changes of the configuration files are still possible.

level   This field is defined for options and for groups. It contains an *unsigned number* that specifies the expert level under which this group or option should be displayed. The following expert levels are defined for options (they have analogous meaning for groups):

basic (0)   This option should always be offered to the user.

advanced (1)
> This option may be offered to advanced users.

expert (2)
> This option should only be offered to expert users.

invisible (3)
> This option should normally never be displayed, not even to expert users.

internal (4)
> This option is for internal use only. Ignore it.

The level of a group will always be the lowest level of all options it contains.

description

    This field is defined for options and groups. The *string* in this field contains a human-readable description of the option or group. It can be displayed to the user of the GUI for informational purposes. It is *percent-escaped* and *localized*.

type   This field is only defined for options. It contains an *unsigned number* that specifies the type of the option's argument, if any. The following types are defined:

Basic types:

none (0)   No argument allowed.

string (1)
>   An *unformatted string*.

int32 (2)   A *signed number*.

uint32 (3)
>   An *unsigned number*.

Complex types:

pathname (32)
>   A *string* that describes the pathname of a file. The file does not necessarily need to exist.

ldap server (33)
>   A *string* that describes an LDAP server in the format:
>
>   *hostname*:*port*:*username*:*password*:*base_dn*

key fingerprint (34)
>   A *string* with a 40 digit fingerprint specifying a certificate.

pub key (35)
>   A *string* that describes a certificate by user ID, key ID or fingerprint.

sec key (36)
>   A *string* that describes a certificate with a key by user ID, key ID or fingerprint.

alias list (37)
>   A *string* that describes an alias list, like the one used with gpg's group option. The list consists of a key, an equal sign and space separated values.

More types will be added in the future. Please see the *alt-type* field for information on how to cope with unknown types.

alt-type   This field is identical to *type*, except that only the types 0 to 31 are allowed. The GUI is expected to present the user the option in the format specified by *type*. But if the argument type *type* is not supported by the GUI, it can still display the option in the more generic basic type *alt-type*. The GUI must support all the defined basic types to be able to display all options. More basic types may be added in future versions. If the GUI encounters a basic type it doesn't support, it should report an error and abort the operation.

argname   This field is only defined for options with an argument type *type* that is not 0. In this case it may contain a *percent-escaped* and *localised string* that gives a short name for the argument. The field may also be empty, though, in which case a short name is not known.

default   This field is defined only for options for which the **default** or **default desc** flag is set. If the **default** flag is set, its format is that of an *option argument*

(See Section 8.4.2 [Format conventions], page 120, for details). If the default value is empty, then no default is known. Otherwise, the value specifies the default value for this option. If the `default desc` flag is set, the field is either empty or contains a description of the effect if the option is not given.

argdef This field is defined only for options for which the `optional arg` flag is set. If the `no arg desc` flag is not set, its format is that of an *option argument* (See Section 8.4.2 [Format conventions], page 120, for details). If the default value is empty, then no default is known. Otherwise, the value specifies the default argument for this option. If the `no arg desc` flag is set, the field is either empty or contains a description of the effect of this option if no argument is given.

value This field is defined only for options. Its format is that of an *option argument*. If it is empty, then the option is not explicitly set in the current configuration, and the default applies (if any). Otherwise, it contains the current value of the option. Note that this field is also meaningful if the option itself does not take a real argument (in this case, it contains the number of times the option appears).

8.4.6 Changing options

The command `--change-options` `component` will attempt to change the options of the component *component* to the specified values. *component* must be the string in the field *name* in the output of the `--list-components` command. You have to provide the options that shall be changed in the following format on standard input:

> *name*:*flags*:*new-value*

name This is the name of the option to change. *name* must be the string in the field *name* in the output of the `--list-options` command.

flags The flags field contains an *unsigned number*. Its value is the OR-wise combination of the following flag values:

> `default (16)`
>
> > If this flag is set, the option is deleted and the default value is used instead (if applicable).

new-value The new value for the option. This field is only defined if the `default` flag is not set. The format is that of an *option argument*. If it is empty (or the field is omitted), the default argument is used (only allowed if the argument is optional for this option). Otherwise, the option will be set to the specified value.

The output of the command is the same as that of `--check-options` for the modified configuration file.

Examples:

To set the force option, which is of basic type `none (0)`:

> `$ echo 'force:0:1' | gpgconf --change-options dirmngr`

To delete the force option:

> `$ echo 'force:16:' | gpgconf --change-options dirmngr`

The `--runtime` option can influence when the changes take effect.

8.4.7 Listing global options

Sometimes it is useful for applications to look at the global options file 'gpgconf.conf'. The colon separated listing format is record oriented and uses the first field to identify the record type:

k   This describes a key record to start the definition of a new ruleset for a user/group. The format of a key record is:

                    `k:`*user*`:`*group*`:`

          user   This is the user field of the key. It is percent escaped. See the definition of the gpgconf.conf format for details.

          group   This is the group field of the key. It is percent escaped.

r   This describes a rule record. All rule records up to the next key record make up a rule set for that key. The format of a rule record is:

                    `r:::`*component*`:`*option*`:`*flags*`:`*value*`:`

          component
                  This is the component part of a rule. It is a plain string.

          option   This is the option part of a rule. It is a plain string.

          flag   This is the flags part of a rule. There may be only one flag per rule but by using the same component and option, several flags may be assigned to an option. It is a plain string.

          value   This is the optional value for the option. It is a percent escaped string with a single quotation mark to indicate a string. The quotation mark is only required to distinguish between no value specified and an empty string.

Unknown record types should be ignored. Note that there is intentionally no feature to change the global option file through `gpgconf`.

8.4.8 Files used by gpgconf

'/etc/gnupg/gpgconf.conf'
                  If this file exists, it is processed as a global configuration file. A commented example can be found in the 'examples' directory of the distribution.

8.5 Run gpgconf for all users.

This script is a wrapper around `gpgconf` to run it with the command `--apply-defaults` for all real users with an existing GnuPG home directory. Admins might want to use this script to update he GnuPG configuration files for all users after '/etc/gnupg/gpgconf.conf' has been changed. This allows to enforce certain policies for all users. Note, that this is not a bulletproof of forcing a user to use certain options. A user may always directly edit the configuration files and bypass gpgconf.

`applygnupgdefaults` is invoked by root as:

    `applygnupgdefaults`

8.6 Put a passphrase into the cache.

The gpg-preset-passphrase is a utility to seed the internal cache of a running gpg-agent with passphrases. It is mainly useful for unattended machines, where the usual pinentry tool may not be used and the passphrases for the to be used keys are given at machine startup.

Passphrases set with this utility don't expire unless the '--forget' option is used to explicitly clear them from the cache — or gpg-agent is either restarted or reloaded (by sending a SIGHUP to it). Note that the maximum cache time as set with '--max-cache-ttl' is still honored. It is necessary to allow this passphrase presetting by starting gpg-agent with the '--allow-preset-passphrase'.

8.6.1 List of all commands and options.

gpg-preset-passphrase is invoked this way:

```
gpg-preset-passphrase [options] [command] cacheid
```

cacheid is either a 40 character keygrip of hexadecimal characters identifying the key for which the passphrase should be set or cleared. The keygrip is listed along with the key when running the command: gpgsm --dump-secret-keys. Alternatively an arbitrary string may be used to identify a passphrase; it is suggested that such a string is prefixed with the name of the application (e.g foo:12346).

One of the following command options must be given:

--preset   Preset a passphrase. This is what you usually will use. gpg-preset-passphrase will then read the passphrase from stdin.

--forget   Flush the passphrase for the given cache ID from the cache.

The following additional options may be used:

-v
--verbose
            Output additional information while running.

-P string
--passphrase string
            Instead of reading the passphrase from stdin, use the supplied string as passphrase. Note that this makes the passphrase visible for other users.

8.7 Communicate with a running agent.

The gpg-connect-agent is a utility to communicate with a running gpg-agent. It is useful to check out the commands gpg-agent provides using the Assuan interface. It might also be useful for scripting simple applications. Input is expected at stdin and out put gets printed to stdout.

It is very similar to running gpg-agent in server mode; but here we connect to a running instance.

8.7.1 List of all options.

`gpg-connect-agent` is invoked this way:

> `gpg-connect-agent [options] [commands]`

The following options may be used:

`-v`

`--verbose`

> Output additional information while running.

`-q`

`--quiet`   Try to be as quiet as possible.

`--homedir` *dir*

> Set the name of the home directory to *dir*. If this option is not used, the home directory defaults to '`~/.gnupg`'. It is only recognized when given on the command line. It also overrides any home directory stated through the environment variable `GNUPGHOME` or (on Windows systems) by means of the Registry entry *HKCU\Software\GNU\GnuPG:HomeDir*.

> On Windows systems it is possible to install GnuPG as a portable application. In this case only this command line option is considered, all other ways to set a home directory are ignored.

> To install GnuPG as a portable application under Windows, create an empty file name '`gpgconf.ctl`' in the same directory as the tool '`gpgconf.exe`'. The root of the installation is than that directory; or, if '`gpgconf.exe`' has been installed directly below a directory named '`bin`', its parent directory. You also need to make sure that the following directories exist and are writable: '`ROOT/home`' for the GnuPG home and '`ROOT/usr/local/var/cache/gnupg`' for internal cache files.

`--agent-program` *file*

> Specify the agent program to be started if none is running. The default value is determined by running `gpgconf` with the option '`--list-dirs`'. Note that the pipe symbol (`|`) is used for a regression test suite hack and may thus not be used in the file name.

`--dirmngr-program` *file*

> Specify the directory manager (keyserver client) program to be started if none is running. This has only an effect if used together with the option '`--dirmngr`'.

`--dirmngr`

> Connect to a running directory manager (keyserver client) instead of to the gpg-agent. If a dirmngr is not running, start it.

`-S`

`--raw-socket` *name*

> Connect to socket *name* assuming this is an Assuan style server. Do not run any special initializations or environment checks. This may be used to directly connect to any Assuan style socket server.

`-E`

`--exec`   Take the rest of the command line as a program and it's arguments and execute it as an assuan server. Here is how you would run `gpgsm`:

> `gpg-connect-agent --exec gpgsm --server`

Note that you may not use options on the command line in this case.

`--no-ext-connect`

When using '`-S`' or '`--exec`', `gpg-connect-agent` connects to the assuan server in extended mode to allow descriptor passing. This option makes it use the old mode.

`--no-autostart`

Do not start the gpg-agent or the dirmngr if it has not yet been started.

`-r file`
`--run file`

Run the commands from *file* at startup and then continue with the regular input method. Note, that commands given on the command line are executed after this file.

`-s`
`--subst`   Run the command `/subst` at startup.

`--hex`   Print data lines in a hex format and the ASCII representation of non-control characters.

`--decode`   Decode data lines. That is to remove percent escapes but make sure that a new line always starts with a D and a space.

8.7.2 Control commands.

While reading Assuan commands, gpg-agent also allows a few special commands to control its operation. These control commands all start with a slash (/).

`/echo args`

Just print *args*.

`/let name value`

Set the variable *name* to *value*. Variables are only substituted on the input if the `/subst` has been used. Variables are referenced by prefixing the name with a dollar sign and optionally include the name in curly braces. The rules for a valid name are identically to those of the standard bourne shell. This is not yet enforced but may be in the future. When used with curly braces no leading or trailing white space is allowed.

If a variable is not found, it is searched in the environment and if found copied to the table of variables.

Variable functions are available: The name of the function must be followed by at least one space and the at least one argument. The following functions are available:

get   Return a value described by the argument. Available arguments are:

cwd   The current working directory.

homedir   The gnupg homedir.

sysconfdir
            GnuPG's system configuration directory.

bindir   GnuPG's binary directory.

libdir   GnuPG's library directory.

libexecdir
            GnuPG's library directory for executable files.

datadir   GnuPG's data directory.

serverpid
            The PID of the current server. Command /serverpid
            must have been given to return a useful value.

unescape *args*
            Remove C-style escapes from *args*. Note that \0 and \x00 ter-
            minate the returned string implicitly. The string to be converted
            are the entire arguments right behind the delimiting space of the
            function name.

unpercent *args*
unpercent+ *args*
            Remove percent style escaping from *args*. Note that %00 terminates
            the string implicitly. The string to be converted are the entire
            arguments right behind the delimiting space of the function name.
            unpercent+ also maps plus signs to a spaces.

percent *args*
percent+ *args*
            Escape the *args* using percent style escaping. Tabs, formfeeds, line-
            feeds, carriage returns and colons are escaped. percent+ also maps
            spaces to plus signs.

errcode *arg*
errsource *arg*
errstring *arg*
            Assume *arg* is an integer and evaluate it using strtol. Return the
            gpg-error error code, error source or a formatted string with the
            error code and error source.

+
−
*
/
%   Evaluate all arguments as long integers using strtol and apply
            this operator. A division by zero yields an empty string.

!	
&	Evaluate all arguments as long integers using `strtol` and apply the logical operators NOT, OR or AND. The NOT operator works on the last argument only.

/definq *name var*

Use content of the variable *var* for inquiries with *name*. *name* may be an asterisk (*) to match any inquiry.

/definqfile *name file*

Use content of *file* for inquiries with *name*. *name* may be an asterisk (*) to match any inquiry.

/definqprog *name prog*

Run *prog* for inquiries matching *name* and pass the entire line to it as command line arguments.

/datafile *name*

Write all data lines from the server to the file *name*. The file is opened for writing and created if it does not exists. An existing file is first truncated to 0. The data written to the file fully decoded. Using a single dash for *name* writes to stdout. The file is kept open until a new file is set using this command or this command is used without an argument.

/showdef   Print all definitions

/cleardef

Delete all definitions

/sendfd *file mode*

Open *file* in *mode* (which needs to be a valid `fopen` mode string) and send the file descriptor to the server. This is usually followed by a command like `INPUT FD` to set the input source for other commands.

/recvfd   Not yet implemented.

/open *var file* [*mode*]

Open *file* and assign the file descriptor to *var*. Warning: This command is experimental and might change in future versions.

/close *fd*

Close the file descriptor *fd*. Warning: This command is experimental and might change in future versions.

/showopen

Show a list of open files.

/serverpid

Send the Assuan command `GETINFO pid` to the server and store the returned PID for internal purposes.

/sleep   Sleep for a second.

/hex

/nohex   Same as the command line option '`--hex`'.

/decode

/nodecode

              Same as the command line option '`--decode`'.

/subst

/nosubst   Enable and disable variable substitution. It defaults to disabled unless the command line option '`--subst`' has been used. If /subst as been enabled once, leading whitespace is removed from input lines which makes scripts easier to read.

/while *condition*

/end   These commands provide a way for executing loops. All lines between the `while` and the corresponding `end` are executed as long as the evaluation of *condition* yields a non-zero value or is the string `true` or `yes`. The evaluation is done by passing *condition* to the `strtol` function. Example:

```
/subst
/let i 3
/while $i
  /echo loop couter is $i
  /let i ${- $i 1}
/end
```

/if *condition*

/end   These commands provide a way for conditional execution. All lines between the `if` and the corresponding `end` are executed only if the evaluation of *condition* yields a non-zero value or is the string `true` or `yes`. The evaluation is done by passing *condition* to the `strtol` function.

/run *file*

              Run commands from *file*.

/bye   Terminate the connection and the program

/help   Print a list of available control commands.

8.8 The Dirmngr Client Tool

The `dirmngr-client` is a simple tool to contact a running dirmngr and test whether a certificate has been revoked — either by being listed in the corresponding CRL or by running the OCSP protocol. If no dirmngr is running, a new instances will be started but this is in general not a good idea due to the huge performance overhead.

The usual way to run this tool is either:

        dirmngr-client *acert*

or

        dirmngr-client <*acert*

Where *acert* is one DER encoded (binary) X.509 certificates to be tested. The return value of this command is

0   The certificate under question is valid; i.e. there is a valid CRL available and it
                is not listed tehre or teh OCSP request returned that that certificate is valid.

1   The certificate has been revoked

2 (and other values)
                There was a problem checking the revocation state of the certificate. A message
                to stderr has given more detailed information. Most likely this is due to a
                missing or expired CRL or due to a network problem.

`dirmngr-client` may be called with the following options:

`--version`
                Print the program version and licensing information. Note that you cannot
                abbreviate this command.

`--help, -h`
                Print a usage message summarizing the most useful command-line options.
                Note that you cannot abbreviate this command.

`--quiet, -q`
                Make the output extra brief by suppressing any informational messages.

`-v`

`--verbose`
                Outputs additional information while running. You can increase the verbosity
                by giving several verbose commands to DIRMNGR, such as '-vv'.

`--pem`   Assume that the given certificate is in PEM (armored) format.

`--ocsp`   Do the check using the OCSP protocol and ignore any CRLs.

`--force-default-responder`
                When checking using the OCSP protocl, force the use of the default OCSP
                responder. That is not to use the Reponder as given by the certificate.

`--ping`   Check whether the dirmngr daemon is up and running.

`--cache-cert`
                Put the given certificate into the cache of a running dirmngr. This is mainly
                useful for debugging.

`--validate`
                Validate the given certificate using dirmngr's internal validation code. This is
                mainly useful for debugging.

`--load-crl`
                This command expects a list of filenames with DER encoded CRL files. With
                the option '--url' URLs are expected in place of filenames and they are loaded
                directly from the given location. All CRLs will be validated and then loaded
                into dirmngr's cache.

`--lookup`   Take the remaining arguments and run a lookup command on each of them.
                The results are Base-64 encoded outputs (without header lines). This may be
                used to retrieve certificates from a server. However the output format is not
                very well suited if more than one certificate is returned.

```
--url
-u            Modify the lookup and load-crl commands to take an URL.

--local
-l            Let the lookup command only search the local cache.

--squid-mode
```
Run DIRMNGR-CLIENT in a mode suitable as a helper program for Squid's 'external_acl_type' option.

8.9 Parse a mail message into an annotated format

The gpgparsemail is a utility currently only useful for debugging. Run it with --help for usage information.

8.10 Call a simple symmetric encryption tool.

Sometimes simple encryption tools are already in use for a long time and there might be a desire to integrate them into the GnuPG framework. The protocols and encryption methods might be non-standard or not even properly documented, so that a full-fledged encryption tool with an interface like gpg is not doable. symcryptrun provides a solution: It operates by calling the external encryption/decryption module and provides a passphrase for a key using the standard pinentry based mechanism through gpg-agent.

Note, that symcryptrun is only available if GnuPG has been configured with '--enable-symcryptrun' at build time.

8.10.1 List of all commands and options.

symcryptrun is invoked this way:

```
symcryptrun --class CLASS --program PROGRAM --keyfile KEYFILE
    [--decrypt | --encrypt] [inputfile]
```

For encryption, the plain text must be provided on STDIN or as the argument *inputfile*, and the ciphertext will be output to STDOUT. For decryption vice versa.

CLASS describes the calling conventions of the external tool. Currently it must be given as 'confucius'. *PROGRAM* is the full filename of that external tool.

For the class 'confucius' the option '--keyfile' is required; *keyfile* is the name of a file containing the secret key, which may be protected by a passphrase. For detailed calling conventions, see the source code.

Note, that gpg-agent must be running before starting symcryptrun.

The following additional options may be used:

```
-v
--verbose
```
Output additional information while running.

```
-q
--quiet       Try to be as quiet as possible.
```

`--homedir` *dir*

> Set the name of the home directory to *dir*. If this option is not used, the home directory defaults to '`~/.gnupg`'. It is only recognized when given on the command line. It also overrides any home directory stated through the environment variable `GNUPGHOME` or (on Windows systems) by means of the Registry entry *HKCU\Software\GNU\GnuPG:HomeDir*.
>
> On Windows systems it is possible to install GnuPG as a portable application. In this case only this command line option is considered, all other ways to set a home directory are ignored.
>
> To install GnuPG as a portable application under Windows, create an empty file name '`gpgconf.ctl`' in the same directory as the tool '`gpgconf.exe`'. The root of the installation is than that directory; or, if '`gpgconf.exe`' has been installed directly below a directory named '`bin`', its parent directory. You also need to make sure that the following directories exist and are writable: '`ROOT/home`' for the GnuPG home and '`ROOT/usr/local/var/cache/gnupg`' for internal cache files.

`--log-file` *file*

> Append all logging output to *file*. Default is to write logging information to STDERR.

The possible exit status codes of `symcryptrun` are:

0   Success.

1   Some error occured.

2   No valid passphrase was provided.

3   The operation was canceled by the user.

8.11 Encrypt or sign files into an archive

`gpg-zip` encrypts or signs files into an archive. It is an gpg-ized tar using the same format as used by PGP's PGP Zip.

`gpg-zip` is invoked this way:

    gpg-zip [options] *filename1* [*filename2*, ...] *directory* [*directory2*, ...]

`gpg-zip` understands these options:

`--encrypt`
`-e`   Encrypt data. This option may be combined with '`--symmetric`' (for output that may be decrypted via a secret key or a passphrase).

`--decrypt`
`-d`   Decrypt data.

`--symmetric`
`-c`   Encrypt with a symmetric cipher using a passphrase. The default symmetric cipher used is CAST5, but may be chosen with the '`--cipher-algo`' option to `gpg`.

`--sign`

`-s`   Make a signature. See **gpg**.

`--recipient` *user*

`-r` *user*   Encrypt for user id *user*. See **gpg**.

`--local-user` *user*

`-u` *user*   Use *user* as the key to sign with. See **gpg**.

`--list-archive`

          List the contents of the specified archive.

`--output` *file*

`-o` *file*   Write output to specified file *file*.

`--gpg` *gpgcmd*

          Use the specified command *gpgcmd* instead of **gpg**.

`--gpg-args` *args*

          Pass the specified options to **gpg**.

`--tar` *tarcmd*

          Use the specified command *tarcmd* instead of **tar**.

`--tar-args` *args*

          Pass the specified options to **tar**.

`--version`

          Print version of the program and exit.

`--help`   Display a brief help page and exit.

The program returns 0 if everything was fine, 1 otherwise.

Some examples:

Encrypt the contents of directory 'mydocs' for user Bob to file 'test1':

        gpg-zip --encrypt --output test1 --gpg-args -r Bob mydocs

List the contents of archive 'test1':

        gpg-zip --list-archive test1

9 How to do certain things

This is a collection of small howto documents.

9.1 Creating a TLS server certificate

Here is a brief run up on how to create a server certificate. It has actually been done this way to get a certificate from CAcert to be used on a real server. It has only been tested with this CA, but there shouldn't be any problem to run this against any other CA.

We start by generating an X.509 certificate signing request. As there is no need for a configuration file, you may simply enter:

```
$ gpgsm --gen-key >example.com.cert-req.pem
Please select what kind of key you want:
   (1) RSA
   (2) Existing key
   (3) Existing key from card
Your selection? 1
```

I opted for creating a new RSA key. The other option is to use an already existing key, by selecting 2 and entering the so-called keygrip. Running the command 'gpgsm --dump-secret-key USERID' shows you this keygrip. Using 3 offers another menu to create a certificate directly from a smart card based key.

Let's continue:

```
What keysize do you want? (2048)
Requested keysize is 2048 bits
```

Hitting enter chooses the default RSA key size of 2048 bits. Smaller keys are too weak on the modern Internet. If you choose a larger (stronger) key, your server will need to do more work.

```
Possible actions for a RSA key:
   (1) sign, encrypt
   (2) sign
   (3) encrypt
Your selection? 1
```

Selecting "sign" enables use of the key for Diffie-Hellman key exchange mechanisms (DHE and ECDHE) in TLS, which are preferred because they offer forward secrecy. Selecting "encrypt" enables RSA key exchange mechanisms, which are still common in some places. Selecting both enables both key exchange mechanisms.

Now for some real data:

```
Enter the X.509 subject name: CN=example.com
```

This is the most important value for a server certificate. Enter here the canonical name of your server machine. You may add other virtual server names later.

```
E-Mail addresses (end with an empty line):
>
```

We don't need email addresses in a TLS server certificate and CAcert would anyway ignore such a request. Thus just hit enter.

If you want to create a client certificate for email encryption, this would be the place to enter your mail address (e.g. joe@example.org). You may enter as many addresses as you like, however the CA may not accept them all or reject the entire request.

```
Enter DNS names (optional; end with an empty line):
> example.com
> www.example.com
>
```

Here I entered the names of the services which the machine actually provides. You almost always want to include the canonical name here too. The browser will accept a certificate for any of these names. As usual the CA must approve all of these names.

```
URIs (optional; end with an empty line):
>
```

It is possible to insert arbitrary URIs into a certificate; for a server certificate this does not make sense.

```
Create self-signed certificate? (y/N)
```

Since we are creating a certificate signing request, and not a full certificate, we answer no here, or just hit enter for the default.

We have now entered all required information and **gpgsm** will display what it has gathered and ask whether to create the certificate request:

```
These parameters are used:
    Key-Type: RSA
    Key-Length: 2048
    Key-Usage: sign, encrypt
    Name-DN: CN=example.com
    Name-DNS: example.com
    Name-DNS: www.example.com

Proceed with creation? (y/N) y
```

gpgsm will now start working on creating the request. As this includes the creation of an RSA key it may take a while. During this time you will be asked 3 times for a passphrase to protect the created private key on your system. A pop up window will appear to ask for it. The first two prompts are for the new passphrase and for re-entering it; the third one is required to actually create the certificate signing request.

When it is ready, you should see the final notice:

```
gpgsm: certificate request created
Ready.  You should now send this request to your CA.
```

Now, you may look at the created request:

```
$ cat example.com.cert-req.pem
-----BEGIN CERTIFICATE REQUEST-----
MIIClTCCAX0CAQAwFjEUMBIGA1UEAxMLZXhhbXBsZS5jb20wggEiMA0GCSqGSIb3
DQEBAQUAA4IBDwAwggEKAoIBAQDP1QEcbTvOLLCX4gAoOzH9AW7jNOMj7OSOLOuW
h2bCdkK5YVpnX212Z6COTC3ZG0pJiCeGt1TbbDJUlTa4syQ6JXavjK66N8ASZsyC
Rwcl0m6hbXp541t1dbgt2VgeGk25okWw3j+brw6zxLD2TnthJxOatID01DIG47HW
GqzZmA6WHbIBIONmGnReIHTpPAPCDm92vUkpKG1xLPszuRmsQbwEl870W/FHrsvm
DPvVUUSdIvTV9NuRt7/WY6G4nPp9QlIuTf1ESPzIuIE91gKPdrRCAxOyuT708S1n
xCv3ETQ/bKPoAQ67eE3mPBqkcVwv9SE/2/36Lz06kAizRgs5AgMBAAGgOjA4Bgkq
hkiG9w0BCQ4xKzApMCcGA1UdEQQgMB6CC2V4YW1wbGUuY29tgg93d3cuZXhhbXBs
ZS5jb20wDQYJKoZIhvcNAQELBQADggEBAEWD0Qqz4OENLYp6yyO/KqFOig9FDsLN
b5/R+qhms5qlhdB5+Dh+j693SjOUgbcNKc6JT86IuBqEBZmRCJuXRoKoo5aMS1cJ
hXga7N9IA3qb4VBUzBWvlL92U2Iptr/cEbikFlYZF2Zv3PBv8RfopVlI3OLbKV9D
bJJTt/6kuoydXKo/Vx4GODFzIKNdFdJk86o/Ziz8NOs9JjZxw9H9VY5sHKFM5LKk
VcLwnnLR1NjBGB+9VK/Tze575eGOcJomTp7UGIB+1xzIQVAhUZOizRDv9tHDeaK3
k+tUhVOkuJcYHucpJycDSrP/uAY5zuVJOrs2QSjdnav62YrRgEsxJrU=
-----END CERTIFICATE REQUEST-----
$
```

You may now proceed by logging into your account at the CAcert website, choose Server Certificates – New, check sign by class 3 root certificate, paste the above request block into the text field and click on Submit.

If everything works out fine, a certificate will be shown. Now run

```
$ gpgsm --import
```

and paste the certificate from the CAcert page into your terminal followed by a Ctrl-D

```
-----BEGIN CERTIFICATE-----
MIIEIjCCAgqgAwIBAgIBTDANBgkqhkiG9w0BAQQFADBUMRQwEgYDVQQKEwtDQWN1
  [...]
rUTFlNElRXCwIl0YcJkIaYYqWf7+A/aqYJCi8+51usZwMy3Jsq3hJ6MA3h1BgwZs
Rtct3tIX
-----END CERTIFICATE-----
gpgsm: issuer certificate (#/CN=CAcert Class 3 Ro[...]) not found
gpgsm: certificate imported

gpgsm: total number processed: 1
gpgsm:                 imported: 1
```

gpgsm tells you that it has imported the certificate. It is now associated with the key
you used when creating the request. The root certificate has not been found, so you may
want to import it from the CACert website.

To see the content of your certificate, you may now enter:

```
$ gpgsm -K example.com
/home/foo/.gnupg/pubring.kbx
-------------------------
Serial number: 4C
       Issuer: /CN=CAcert Class 3 Root/OU=http:\x2f\x2fwww.[...]
      Subject: /CN=example.com
          aka: (dns-name example.com)
          aka: (dns-name www.example.com)
     validity: 2015-07-01 16:20:51 through 2016-07-01 16:20:51
     key type: 2048 bit RSA
    key usage: digitalSignature keyEncipherment
ext key usage: clientAuth (suggested), serverAuth (suggested), [...]
  fingerprint: 0F:9C:27:B2:DA:05:5F:CB:33:D8:19:E9:65:B9:4F:BD:B1:98:CC:57
```

I used '-K' above because this will only list certificates for which a private key is available.
To see more details, you may use '--dump-secret-keys' instead of '-K'.

To make actual use of the certificate you need to install it on your server. Server software
usually expects a PKCS\#12 file with key and certificate. To create such a file, run:

```
$ gpgsm --export-secret-key-p12 -a >example.com-cert.pem
```

You will be asked for the passphrase as well as for a new passphrase to be used to protect
the PKCS\#12 file. The file now contains the certificate as well as the private key:

```
$ cat example-cert.pem
Issuer ...: /CN=CAcert Class 3 Root/OU=http:\x2f\x2fwww.CA[...]
Serial ...: 4C
Subject ..: /CN=example.com
    aka ..: (dns-name example.com)
    aka ..: (dns-name www.example.com)


-----BEGIN PKCS12-----
MIIHlwIBAzCCB5AGCSqGSIb37QdHAaCCB4EEggd9MIIHeTk1BJ8GCSqGSIb3DQEu
[...many more lines...]
-----END PKCS12-----
$
```

Copy this file in a secure way to the server, install it there and delete the file then. You may export the file again at any time as long as it is available in GnuPG's private key database.

10 Notes pertaining to certain OSes.

GnuPG has been developed on GNU/Linux systems and is know to work on almost all Free OSes. All modern POSIX systems should be supported right now, however there are probably a lot of smaller glitches we need to fix first. The major problem areas are:

- For logging to sockets and other internal operations the `fopencookie` function (`funopen` under *BSD) is used. This is a very convenient function which makes it possible to create outputs in a structures and easy maintainable way. The drawback however is that most proprietary OSes don't support this function. At g10 Code we have looked into several ways on how to overcome this limitation but no sufficiently easy and maintainable way has been found. Porting *glibc* to a general POSIX system is of course an option and would make writing portable software much easier; this it has not yet been done and the system administrator would need to cope with the GNU specific admin things in addition to the generic ones of his system.

  We have now settled to use explicit stdio wrappers with a functionality similar to funopen. Although the code for this has already been written (*libestream*), we have not yet changed GnuPG to use it.

  This means that on systems not supporting either `funopen` or `fopencookie`, logging to a socket won't work, prompts are not formatted as pretty as they should be and `gpgsm`'s `LISTKEYS` Assuan command does not work.

- We are planning to use file descriptor passing for interprocess communication. This will allow us save a lot of resources and improve performance of certain operations a lot. Systems not supporting this won't gain these benefits but we try to keep them working the standard way as it is done today.

- We require more or less full POSIX compatibility. This has been around for 15 years now and thus we don't believe it makes sense to support non POSIX systems anymore. Well, we of course the usual workarounds for near POSIX systems well be applied.

  There is one exception of this rule: Systems based the Microsoft Windows API (called here *W32*) will be supported to some extend.

10.1 Microsoft Windows Notes

Current limitations are:

- `gpgconf` does not create backup files, so in case of trouble your configuration file might get lost.

- `watchgnupg` is not available. Logging to sockets is not possible.

- The periodical smartcard status checking done by `scdaemon` is not yet supported.

11 How to solve problems

Everyone knows that software often does not do what it should do and thus there is a need to track down problems. We call this debugging in a reminiscent to the moth jamming a relay in a Mark II box back in 1947.

Most of the problems a merely configuration and user problems but nevertheless there are the most annoying ones and responsible for many gray hairs. We try to give some guidelines here on how to identify and solve the problem at hand.

11.1 Debugging Tools

The GnuPG distribution comes with a couple of tools, useful to help find and solving problems.

11.1.1 Scrutinizing a keybox file

A keybox is a file format used to store public keys along with meta information and indices. The commonly used one is the file 'pubring.kbx' in the '.gnupg' directory. It contains all X.509 certificates as well as OpenPGP keys[1] .

When called the standard way, e.g.:

'kbxutil ~/.gnupg/pubring.kbx'

it lists all records (called blobs) with there meta-information in a human readable format.

To see statistics on the keybox in question, run it using

'kbxutil --stats ~/.gnupg/pubring.kbx'

and you get an output like:

```
Total number of blobs:        99
             header:           1
              empty:           0
            openpgp:           0
               x509:          98
        non flagged:          81
     secret flagged:           0
   ephemeral flagged:         17
```

In this example you see that the keybox does not have any OpenPGP keys but contains 98 X.509 certificates and a total of 17 keys or certificates are flagged as ephemeral, meaning that they are only temporary stored (cached) in the keybox and won't get listed using the usual commands provided by **gpgsm** or **gpg**. 81 certificates are stored in a standard way and directly available from **gpgsm**.

To find duplicated certificates and keyblocks in a keybox file (this should not occur but sometimes things go wrong), run it using

'kbxutil --find-dups ~/.gnupg/pubring.kbx'

---

[1] Well, OpenPGP keys are not implemented, **gpg** still used the keyring file 'pubring.gpg'

11.2 Various hints on debugging.

- How to find the IP address of a keyserver

  If a round robin URL of is used for a keyserver (e.g. subkeys.gnupg.org); it is not easy
  to see what server is actually used. Using the keyserver debug option as in

  ```
  gpg --keyserver-options debug=1 -v --refresh-key 1E42B367
  ```

  is thus often helpful. Note that the actual output depends on the backend and may
  change from release to release.

- Logging on WindowsCE

  For development, the best logging method on WindowsCE is the use of remote debugging using a log file name of 'tcp://<ip-addr>:<port>'. The command watchgnupg
  may be used on the remote host to listen on the given port. (see [option watchgnupg
  –tcp], page 115). For in the field tests it is better to make use of the logging facility
  provided by the gpgcedev driver (part of libassuan); this is enabled by using a log file
  name of 'GPG2:'. (see [option –log-file], page 6).

11.3 Commonly Seen Problems

- Error code 'Not supported' from Dirmngr

  Most likely the option 'enable-ocsp' is active for gpgsm but Dirmngr's OCSP feature
  has not been enabled using 'allow-ocsp' in 'dirmngr.conf'.

- The Curses based Pinentry does not work

  The far most common reason for this is that the environment variable GPG_TTY has not
  been set correctly. Make sure that it has been set to a real tty devce and not just to
  '/dev/tty'; i.e. 'GPG_TTY=tty' is plainly wrong; what you want is 'GPG_TTY=`tty`' —
  note the back ticks. Also make sure that this environment variable gets exported, that
  is you should follow up the setting with an 'export GPG_TTY' (assuming a Bourne style
  shell). Even for GUI based Pinentries; you should have set GPG_TTY. See the section
  on installing the gpg-agent on how to do it.

- SSH hangs while a popping up pinentry was expected

  SSH has no way to tell the gpg-agent what terminal or X display it is running on. So
  when remotely logging into a box where a gpg-agent with SSH support is running, the
  pinentry will get popped up on whatever display the gpg-agent has been started. To
  solve this problem you may issue the command

  ```
  echo UPDATESTARTUPTTY | gpg-connect-agent
  ```

  and the next pinentry will pop up on your display or screen. However, you need to kill
  the running pinentry first because only one pinentry may be running at once. If you
  plan to use ssh on a new display you should issue the above command before invoking
  ssh or any other service making use of ssh.

- Exporting a secret key without a certificate

  I may happen that you have created a certificate request using gpgsm but not yet
  received and imported the certificate from the CA. However, you want to export the
  secret key to another machine right now to import the certificate over there then. You
  can do this with a little trick but it requires that you know the approximate time you
  created the signing request. By running the command

```
ls -ltr ~/.gnupg/private-keys-v1.d
```

you get a listing of all private keys under control of **gpg-agent**. Pick the key which best matches the creation time and run the command

```
/usr/local/libexec/gpg-protect-tool --p12-export \
    ~/.gnupg/private-keys-v1.d/foo >foo.p12
```

(Please adjust the path to **gpg-protect-tool** to the appropriate location). *foo* is the name of the key file you picked (it should have the suffix '.key'). A Pinentry box will pop up and ask you for the current passphrase of the key and a new passphrase to protect it in the pkcs#12 file.

To import the created file on the machine you use this command:

```
/usr/local/libexec/gpg-protect-tool --p12-import --store  foo.p12
```

You will be asked for the pkcs#12 passphrase and a new passphrase to protect the imported private key at its new location.

Note that there is no easy way to match existing certificates with stored private keys because some private keys are used for Secure Shell or other purposes and don't have a corresponding certificate.

- A root certificate does not verify

  A common problem is that the root certificate misses the required basicConstraints attribute and thus **gpgsm** rejects this certificate. An error message indicating "no value" is a sign for such a certificate. You may use the **relax** flag in 'trustlist.txt' to accept the certificate anyway. Note that the fingerprint and this flag may only be added manually to 'trustlist.txt'.

- Error message: "digest algorithm N has not been enabled"

  The signature is broken. You may try the option '--extra-digest-algo SHA256' to workaround the problem. The number N is the internal algorithm identifier; for example 8 refers to SHA-256.

- The Windows version does not work under Wine

  When running the W32 version of **gpg** under Wine you may get an error messages like:

    `gpg: fatal: WriteConsole failed: Access denied`

  The solution is to use the command **wineconsole**.

  Some operations like gen-key really want to talk to the console directly for increased security (for example to prevent the passphrase from appearing on the screen). So, you should use **wineconsole** instead of **wine**, which will launch a windows console that implements those additional features.

- Why does GPG's –search-key list weird keys?

  For performance reasons the keyservers do not check the keys the same way **gpg** does. It may happen that the listing of keys available on the keyservers shows keys with wrong user IDs or with user Ids from other keys. If you try to import this key, the bad keys or bad user ids won't get imported, though. This is a bit unfortunate but we can't do anything about it without actually downloading the keys.

11.4 How the whole thing works internally.

11.4.1 Relationship between the two branches.

Here is a little picture showing how the components work together:

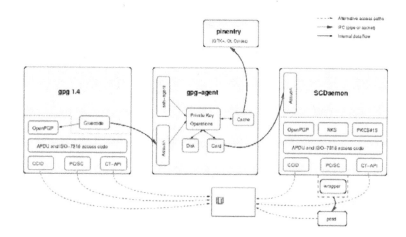

Lets try to explain it:

TO BE DONE.

GNU General Public License

Version 3, 29 June 2007

Copyright © 2007 Free Software Foundation, Inc. http://fsf.org/

Everyone is permitted to copy and distribute verbatim copies of this license document, but changing it is not allowed.

Preamble

The GNU General Public License is a free, copyleft license for software and other kinds of works.

The licenses for most software and other practical works are designed to take away your freedom to share and change the works. By contrast, the GNU General Public License is intended to guarantee your freedom to share and change all versions of a program–to make sure it remains free software for all its users. We, the Free Software Foundation, use the GNU General Public License for most of our software; it applies also to any other work released this way by its authors. You can apply it to your programs, too.

When we speak of free software, we are referring to freedom, not price. Our General Public Licenses are designed to make sure that you have the freedom to distribute copies of free software (and charge for them if you wish), that you receive source code or can get it if you want it, that you can change the software or use pieces of it in new free programs, and that you know you can do these things.

To protect your rights, we need to prevent others from denying you these rights or asking you to surrender the rights. Therefore, you have certain responsibilities if you distribute copies of the software, or if you modify it: responsibilities to respect the freedom of others.

For example, if you distribute copies of such a program, whether gratis or for a fee, you must pass on to the recipients the same freedoms that you received. You must make sure that they, too, receive or can get the source code. And you must show them these terms so they know their rights.

Developers that use the GNU GPL protect your rights with two steps: (1) assert copyright on the software, and (2) offer you this License giving you legal permission to copy, distribute and/or modify it.

For the developers' and authors' protection, the GPL clearly explains that there is no warranty for this free software. For both users' and authors' sake, the GPL requires that modified versions be marked as changed, so that their problems will not be attributed erroneously to authors of previous versions.

Some devices are designed to deny users access to install or run modified versions of the software inside them, although the manufacturer can do so. This is fundamentally incompatible with the aim of protecting users' freedom to change the software. The systematic pattern of such abuse occurs in the area of products for individuals to use, which is precisely where it is most unacceptable. Therefore, we have designed this version of the GPL to prohibit the practice for those products. If such problems arise substantially in other domains, we stand ready to extend this provision to those domains in future versions of the GPL, as needed to protect the freedom of users.

Finally, every program is threatened constantly by software patents. States should not allow patents to restrict development and use of software on general-purpose computers, but in those that do, we wish to avoid the special danger that patents applied to a free program could make it effectively proprietary. To prevent this, the GPL assures that patents cannot be used to render the program non-free.

The precise terms and conditions for copying, distribution and modification follow.

TERMS AND CONDITIONS

0. Definitions.

   "This License" refers to version 3 of the GNU General Public License.

   "Copyright" also means copyright-like laws that apply to other kinds of works, such as semiconductor masks.

   "The Program" refers to any copyrightable work licensed under this License. Each licensee is addressed as "you". "Licensees" and "recipients" may be individuals or organizations.

   To "modify" a work means to copy from or adapt all or part of the work in a fashion requiring copyright permission, other than the making of an exact copy. The resulting work is called a "modified version" of the earlier work or a work "based on" the earlier work.

   A "covered work" means either the unmodified Program or a work based on the Program.

   To "propagate" a work means to do anything with it that, without permission, would make you directly or secondarily liable for infringement under applicable copyright law, except executing it on a computer or modifying a private copy. Propagation includes copying, distribution (with or without modification), making available to the public, and in some countries other activities as well.

   To "convey" a work means any kind of propagation that enables other parties to make or receive copies. Mere interaction with a user through a computer network, with no transfer of a copy, is not conveying.

   An interactive user interface displays "Appropriate Legal Notices" to the extent that it includes a convenient and prominently visible feature that (1) displays an appropriate copyright notice, and (2) tells the user that there is no warranty for the work (except to the extent that warranties are provided), that licensees may convey the work under this License, and how to view a copy of this License. If the interface presents a list of user commands or options, such as a menu, a prominent item in the list meets this criterion.

1. Source Code.

   The "source code" for a work means the preferred form of the work for making modifications to it. "Object code" means any non-source form of a work.

   A "Standard Interface" means an interface that either is an official standard defined by a recognized standards body, or, in the case of interfaces specified for a particular programming language, one that is widely used among developers working in that language.

The "System Libraries" of an executable work include anything, other than the work as a whole, that (a) is included in the normal form of packaging a Major Component, but which is not part of that Major Component, and (b) serves only to enable use of the work with that Major Component, or to implement a Standard Interface for which an implementation is available to the public in source code form. A "Major Component", in this context, means a major essential component (kernel, window system, and so on) of the specific operating system (if any) on which the executable work runs, or a compiler used to produce the work, or an object code interpreter used to run it.

The "Corresponding Source" for a work in object code form means all the source code needed to generate, install, and (for an executable work) run the object code and to modify the work, including scripts to control those activities. However, it does not include the work's System Libraries, or general-purpose tools or generally available free programs which are used unmodified in performing those activities but which are not part of the work. For example, Corresponding Source includes interface definition files associated with source files for the work, and the source code for shared libraries and dynamically linked subprograms that the work is specifically designed to require, such as by intimate data communication or control flow between those subprograms and other parts of the work.

The Corresponding Source need not include anything that users can regenerate automatically from other parts of the Corresponding Source.

The Corresponding Source for a work in source code form is that same work.

2. Basic Permissions.

All rights granted under this License are granted for the term of copyright on the Program, and are irrevocable provided the stated conditions are met. This License explicitly affirms your unlimited permission to run the unmodified Program. The output from running a covered work is covered by this License only if the output, given its content, constitutes a covered work. This License acknowledges your rights of fair use or other equivalent, as provided by copyright law.

You may make, run and propagate covered works that you do not convey, without conditions so long as your license otherwise remains in force. You may convey covered works to others for the sole purpose of having them make modifications exclusively for you, or provide you with facilities for running those works, provided that you comply with the terms of this License in conveying all material for which you do not control copyright. Those thus making or running the covered works for you must do so exclusively on your behalf, under your direction and control, on terms that prohibit them from making any copies of your copyrighted material outside their relationship with you.

Conveying under any other circumstances is permitted solely under the conditions stated below. Sublicensing is not allowed; section 10 makes it unnecessary.

3. Protecting Users' Legal Rights From Anti-Circumvention Law.

No covered work shall be deemed part of an effective technological measure under any applicable law fulfilling obligations under article 11 of the WIPO copyright treaty adopted on 20 December 1996, or similar laws prohibiting or restricting circumvention of such measures.

When you convey a covered work, you waive any legal power to forbid circumvention of technological measures to the extent such circumvention is effected by exercising rights under this License with respect to the covered work, and you disclaim any intention to limit operation or modification of the work as a means of enforcing, against the work's users, your or third parties' legal rights to forbid circumvention of technological measures.

4. Conveying Verbatim Copies.

You may convey verbatim copies of the Program's source code as you receive it, in any medium, provided that you conspicuously and appropriately publish on each copy an appropriate copyright notice; keep intact all notices stating that this License and any non-permissive terms added in accord with section 7 apply to the code; keep intact all notices of the absence of any warranty; and give all recipients a copy of this License along with the Program.

You may charge any price or no price for each copy that you convey, and you may offer support or warranty protection for a fee.

5. Conveying Modified Source Versions.

You may convey a work based on the Program, or the modifications to produce it from the Program, in the form of source code under the terms of section 4, provided that you also meet all of these conditions:

  a. The work must carry prominent notices stating that you modified it, and giving a relevant date.

  b. The work must carry prominent notices stating that it is released under this License and any conditions added under section 7. This requirement modifies the requirement in section 4 to "keep intact all notices".

  c. You must license the entire work, as a whole, under this License to anyone who comes into possession of a copy. This License will therefore apply, along with any applicable section 7 additional terms, to the whole of the work, and all its parts, regardless of how they are packaged. This License gives no permission to license the work in any other way, but it does not invalidate such permission if you have separately received it.

  d. If the work has interactive user interfaces, each must display Appropriate Legal Notices; however, if the Program has interactive interfaces that do not display Appropriate Legal Notices, your work need not make them do so.

A compilation of a covered work with other separate and independent works, which are not by their nature extensions of the covered work, and which are not combined with it such as to form a larger program, in or on a volume of a storage or distribution medium, is called an "aggregate" if the compilation and its resulting copyright are not used to limit the access or legal rights of the compilation's users beyond what the individual works permit. Inclusion of a covered work in an aggregate does not cause this License to apply to the other parts of the aggregate.

6. Conveying Non-Source Forms.

You may convey a covered work in object code form under the terms of sections 4 and 5, provided that you also convey the machine-readable Corresponding Source under the terms of this License, in one of these ways:

a. Convey the object code in, or embodied in, a physical product (including a physical distribution medium), accompanied by the Corresponding Source fixed on a durable physical medium customarily used for software interchange.

b. Convey the object code in, or embodied in, a physical product (including a physical distribution medium), accompanied by a written offer, valid for at least three years and valid for as long as you offer spare parts or customer support for that product model, to give anyone who possesses the object code either (1) a copy of the Corresponding Source for all the software in the product that is covered by this License, on a durable physical medium customarily used for software interchange, for a price no more than your reasonable cost of physically performing this conveying of source, or (2) access to copy the Corresponding Source from a network server at no charge.

c. Convey individual copies of the object code with a copy of the written offer to provide the Corresponding Source. This alternative is allowed only occasionally and noncommercially, and only if you received the object code with such an offer, in accord with subsection 6b.

d. Convey the object code by offering access from a designated place (gratis or for a charge), and offer equivalent access to the Corresponding Source in the same way through the same place at no further charge. You need not require recipients to copy the Corresponding Source along with the object code. If the place to copy the object code is a network server, the Corresponding Source may be on a different server (operated by you or a third party) that supports equivalent copying facilities, provided you maintain clear directions next to the object code saying where to find the Corresponding Source. Regardless of what server hosts the Corresponding Source, you remain obligated to ensure that it is available for as long as needed to satisfy these requirements.

e. Convey the object code using peer-to-peer transmission, provided you inform other peers where the object code and Corresponding Source of the work are being offered to the general public at no charge under subsection 6d.

A separable portion of the object code, whose source code is excluded from the Corresponding Source as a System Library, need not be included in conveying the object code work.

A "User Product" is either (1) a "consumer product", which means any tangible personal property which is normally used for personal, family, or household purposes, or (2) anything designed or sold for incorporation into a dwelling. In determining whether a product is a consumer product, doubtful cases shall be resolved in favor of coverage. For a particular product received by a particular user, "normally used" refers to a typical or common use of that class of product, regardless of the status of the particular user or of the way in which the particular user actually uses, or expects or is expected to use, the product. A product is a consumer product regardless of whether the product has substantial commercial, industrial or non-consumer uses, unless such uses represent the only significant mode of use of the product.

"Installation Information" for a User Product means any methods, procedures, authorization keys, or other information required to install and execute modified versions of a covered work in that User Product from a modified version of its Corresponding Source.

The information must suffice to ensure that the continued functioning of the modified object code is in no case prevented or interfered with solely because modification has been made.

If you convey an object code work under this section in, or with, or specifically for use in, a User Product, and the conveying occurs as part of a transaction in which the right of possession and use of the User Product is transferred to the recipient in perpetuity or for a fixed term (regardless of how the transaction is characterized), the Corresponding Source conveyed under this section must be accompanied by the Installation Information. But this requirement does not apply if neither you nor any third party retains the ability to install modified object code on the User Product (for example, the work has been installed in ROM).

The requirement to provide Installation Information does not include a requirement to continue to provide support service, warranty, or updates for a work that has been modified or installed by the recipient, or for the User Product in which it has been modified or installed. Access to a network may be denied when the modification itself materially and adversely affects the operation of the network or violates the rules and protocols for communication across the network.

Corresponding Source conveyed, and Installation Information provided, in accord with this section must be in a format that is publicly documented (and with an implementation available to the public in source code form), and must require no special password or key for unpacking, reading or copying.

7. Additional Terms.

    "Additional permissions" are terms that supplement the terms of this License by making exceptions from one or more of its conditions. Additional permissions that are applicable to the entire Program shall be treated as though they were included in this License, to the extent that they are valid under applicable law. If additional permissions apply only to part of the Program, that part may be used separately under those permissions, but the entire Program remains governed by this License without regard to the additional permissions.

    When you convey a copy of a covered work, you may at your option remove any additional permissions from that copy, or from any part of it. (Additional permissions may be written to require their own removal in certain cases when you modify the work.) You may place additional permissions on material, added by you to a covered work, for which you have or can give appropriate copyright permission.

    Notwithstanding any other provision of this License, for material you add to a covered work, you may (if authorized by the copyright holders of that material) supplement the terms of this License with terms:

    a. Disclaiming warranty or limiting liability differently from the terms of sections 15 and 16 of this License; or

    b. Requiring preservation of specified reasonable legal notices or author attributions in that material or in the Appropriate Legal Notices displayed by works containing it; or

    c. Prohibiting misrepresentation of the origin of that material, or requiring that modified versions of such material be marked in reasonable ways as different from the original version; or

   d. Limiting the use for publicity purposes of names of licensors or authors of the material; or

   e. Declining to grant rights under trademark law for use of some trade names, trademarks, or service marks; or

   f. Requiring indemnification of licensors and authors of that material by anyone who conveys the material (or modified versions of it) with contractual assumptions of liability to the recipient, for any liability that these contractual assumptions directly impose on those licensors and authors.

All other non-permissive additional terms are considered "further restrictions" within the meaning of section 10. If the Program as you received it, or any part of it, contains a notice stating that it is governed by this License along with a term that is a further restriction, you may remove that term. If a license document contains a further restriction but permits relicensing or conveying under this License, you may add to a covered work material governed by the terms of that license document, provided that the further restriction does not survive such relicensing or conveying.

If you add terms to a covered work in accord with this section, you must place, in the relevant source files, a statement of the additional terms that apply to those files, or a notice indicating where to find the applicable terms.

Additional terms, permissive or non-permissive, may be stated in the form of a separately written license, or stated as exceptions; the above requirements apply either way.

8. Termination.

You may not propagate or modify a covered work except as expressly provided under this License. Any attempt otherwise to propagate or modify it is void, and will automatically terminate your rights under this License (including any patent licenses granted under the third paragraph of section 11).

However, if you cease all violation of this License, then your license from a particular copyright holder is reinstated (a) provisionally, unless and until the copyright holder explicitly and finally terminates your license, and (b) permanently, if the copyright holder fails to notify you of the violation by some reasonable means prior to 60 days after the cessation.

Moreover, your license from a particular copyright holder is reinstated permanently if the copyright holder notifies you of the violation by some reasonable means, this is the first time you have received notice of violation of this License (for any work) from that copyright holder, and you cure the violation prior to 30 days after your receipt of the notice.

Termination of your rights under this section does not terminate the licenses of parties who have received copies or rights from you under this License. If your rights have been terminated and not permanently reinstated, you do not qualify to receive new licenses for the same material under section 10.

9. Acceptance Not Required for Having Copies.

You are not required to accept this License in order to receive or run a copy of the Program. Ancillary propagation of a covered work occurring solely as a consequence of using peer-to-peer transmission to receive a copy likewise does not require acceptance.

However, nothing other than this License grants you permission to propagate or modify any covered work. These actions infringe copyright if you do not accept this License. Therefore, by modifying or propagating a covered work, you indicate your acceptance of this License to do so.

10. Automatic Licensing of Downstream Recipients.

Each time you convey a covered work, the recipient automatically receives a license from the original licensors, to run, modify and propagate that work, subject to this License. You are not responsible for enforcing compliance by third parties with this License.

An "entity transaction" is a transaction transferring control of an organization, or substantially all assets of one, or subdividing an organization, or merging organizations. If propagation of a covered work results from an entity transaction, each party to that transaction who receives a copy of the work also receives whatever licenses to the work the party's predecessor in interest had or could give under the previous paragraph, plus a right to possession of the Corresponding Source of the work from the predecessor in interest, if the predecessor has it or can get it with reasonable efforts.

You may not impose any further restrictions on the exercise of the rights granted or affirmed under this License. For example, you may not impose a license fee, royalty, or other charge for exercise of rights granted under this License, and you may not initiate litigation (including a cross-claim or counterclaim in a lawsuit) alleging that any patent claim is infringed by making, using, selling, offering for sale, or importing the Program or any portion of it.

11. Patents.

A "contributor" is a copyright holder who authorizes use under this License of the Program or a work on which the Program is based. The work thus licensed is called the contributor's "contributor version".

A contributor's "essential patent claims" are all patent claims owned or controlled by the contributor, whether already acquired or hereafter acquired, that would be infringed by some manner, permitted by this License, of making, using, or selling its contributor version, but do not include claims that would be infringed only as a consequence of further modification of the contributor version. For purposes of this definition, "control" includes the right to grant patent sublicenses in a manner consistent with the requirements of this License.

Each contributor grants you a non-exclusive, worldwide, royalty-free patent license under the contributor's essential patent claims, to make, use, sell, offer for sale, import and otherwise run, modify and propagate the contents of its contributor version.

In the following three paragraphs, a "patent license" is any express agreement or commitment, however denominated, not to enforce a patent (such as an express permission to practice a patent or covenant not to sue for patent infringement). To "grant" such a patent license to a party means to make such an agreement or commitment not to enforce a patent against the party.

If you convey a covered work, knowingly relying on a patent license, and the Corresponding Source of the work is not available for anyone to copy, free of charge and under the terms of this License, through a publicly available network server or other readily accessible means, then you must either (1) cause the Corresponding Source to be so available, or (2) arrange to deprive yourself of the benefit of the patent license for this particular work, or (3) arrange, in a manner consistent with the requirements of this License, to extend the patent license to downstream recipients. "Knowingly relying" means you have actual knowledge that, but for the patent license, your conveying the covered work in a country, or your recipient's use of the covered work in a country, would infringe one or more identifiable patents in that country that you have reason to believe are valid.

If, pursuant to or in connection with a single transaction or arrangement, you convey, or propagate by procuring conveyance of, a covered work, and grant a patent license to some of the parties receiving the covered work authorizing them to use, propagate, modify or convey a specific copy of the covered work, then the patent license you grant is automatically extended to all recipients of the covered work and works based on it.

A patent license is "discriminatory" if it does not include within the scope of its coverage, prohibits the exercise of, or is conditioned on the non-exercise of one or more of the rights that are specifically granted under this License. You may not convey a covered work if you are a party to an arrangement with a third party that is in the business of distributing software, under which you make payment to the third party based on the extent of your activity of conveying the work, and under which the third party grants, to any of the parties who would receive the covered work from you, a discriminatory patent license (a) in connection with copies of the covered work conveyed by you (or copies made from those copies), or (b) primarily for and in connection with specific products or compilations that contain the covered work, unless you entered into that arrangement, or that patent license was granted, prior to 28 March 2007.

Nothing in this License shall be construed as excluding or limiting any implied license or other defenses to infringement that may otherwise be available to you under applicable patent law.

12. No Surrender of Others' Freedom.

    If conditions are imposed on you (whether by court order, agreement or otherwise) that contradict the conditions of this License, they do not excuse you from the conditions of this License. If you cannot convey a covered work so as to satisfy simultaneously your obligations under this License and any other pertinent obligations, then as a consequence you may not convey it at all. For example, if you agree to terms that obligate you to collect a royalty for further conveying from those to whom you convey the Program, the only way you could satisfy both those terms and this License would be to refrain entirely from conveying the Program.

13. Use with the GNU Affero General Public License.

    Notwithstanding any other provision of this License, you have permission to link or combine any covered work with a work licensed under version 3 of the GNU Affero General Public License into a single combined work, and to convey the resulting work. The terms of this License will continue to apply to the part which is the covered work, but the special requirements of the GNU Affero General Public License, section 13, concerning interaction through a network will apply to the combination as such.

14. Revised Versions of this License.

The Free Software Foundation may publish revised and/or new versions of the GNU General Public License from time to time. Such new versions will be similar in spirit to the present version, but may differ in detail to address new problems or concerns.

Each version is given a distinguishing version number. If the Program specifies that a certain numbered version of the GNU General Public License "or any later version" applies to it, you have the option of following the terms and conditions either of that numbered version or of any later version published by the Free Software Foundation. If the Program does not specify a version number of the GNU General Public License, you may choose any version ever published by the Free Software Foundation.

If the Program specifies that a proxy can decide which future versions of the GNU General Public License can be used, that proxy's public statement of acceptance of a version permanently authorizes you to choose that version for the Program.

Later license versions may give you additional or different permissions. However, no additional obligations are imposed on any author or copyright holder as a result of your choosing to follow a later version.

15. Disclaimer of Warranty.

THERE IS NO WARRANTY FOR THE PROGRAM, TO THE EXTENT PERMITTED BY APPLICABLE LAW. EXCEPT WHEN OTHERWISE STATED IN WRITING THE COPYRIGHT HOLDERS AND/OR OTHER PARTIES PROVIDE THE PROGRAM "AS IS" WITHOUT WARRANTY OF ANY KIND, EITHER EXPRESSED OR IMPLIED, INCLUDING, BUT NOT LIMITED TO, THE IMPLIED WARRANTIES OF MERCHANTABILITY AND FITNESS FOR A PARTICULAR PURPOSE. THE ENTIRE RISK AS TO THE QUALITY AND PERFORMANCE OF THE PROGRAM IS WITH YOU. SHOULD THE PROGRAM PROVE DEFECTIVE, YOU ASSUME THE COST OF ALL NECESSARY SERVICING, REPAIR OR CORRECTION.

16. Limitation of Liability.

IN NO EVENT UNLESS REQUIRED BY APPLICABLE LAW OR AGREED TO IN WRITING WILL ANY COPYRIGHT HOLDER, OR ANY OTHER PARTY WHO MODIFIES AND/OR CONVEYS THE PROGRAM AS PERMITTED ABOVE, BE LIABLE TO YOU FOR DAMAGES, INCLUDING ANY GENERAL, SPECIAL, INCIDENTAL OR CONSEQUENTIAL DAMAGES ARISING OUT OF THE USE OR INABILITY TO USE THE PROGRAM (INCLUDING BUT NOT LIMITED TO LOSS OF DATA OR DATA BEING RENDERED INACCURATE OR LOSSES SUSTAINED BY YOU OR THIRD PARTIES OR A FAILURE OF THE PROGRAM TO OPERATE WITH ANY OTHER PROGRAMS), EVEN IF SUCH HOLDER OR OTHER PARTY HAS BEEN ADVISED OF THE POSSIBILITY OF SUCH DAMAGES.

17. Interpretation of Sections 15 and 16.

If the disclaimer of warranty and limitation of liability provided above cannot be given local legal effect according to their terms, reviewing courts shall apply local law that most closely approximates an absolute waiver of all civil liability in connection with the Program, unless a warranty or assumption of liability accompanies a copy of the Program in return for a fee.

END OF TERMS AND CONDITIONS

How to Apply These Terms to Your New Programs

If you develop a new program, and you want it to be of the greatest possible use to the public, the best way to achieve this is to make it free software which everyone can redistribute and change under these terms.

To do so, attach the following notices to the program. It is safest to attach them to the start of each source file to most effectively state the exclusion of warranty; and each file should have at least the "copyright" line and a pointer to where the full notice is found.

```
one line to give the program's name and a brief idea of what it does.
Copyright (C) year name of author

This program is free software: you can redistribute it and/or modify
it under the terms of the GNU General Public License as published by
the Free Software Foundation, either version 3 of the License, or (at
your option) any later version.

This program is distributed in the hope that it will be useful, but
WITHOUT ANY WARRANTY; without even the implied warranty of
MERCHANTABILITY or FITNESS FOR A PARTICULAR PURPOSE.  See the GNU
General Public License for more details.

You should have received a copy of the GNU General Public License
along with this program.  If not, see http://www.gnu.org/licenses/.
```

Also add information on how to contact you by electronic and paper mail.

If the program does terminal interaction, make it output a short notice like this when it starts in an interactive mode:

```
program Copyright (C) year name of author
This program comes with ABSOLUTELY NO WARRANTY; for details
type 'show w'.  This is free software, and you are
welcome to redistribute it under certain conditions;
type 'show c' for details.
```

The hypothetical commands 'show w' and 'show c' should show the appropriate parts of the General Public License. Of course, your program's commands might be different; for a GUI interface, you would use an "about box".

You should also get your employer (if you work as a programmer) or school, if any, to sign a "copyright disclaimer" for the program, if necessary. For more information on this, and how to apply and follow the GNU GPL, see http://www.gnu.org/licenses/.

The GNU General Public License does not permit incorporating your program into proprietary programs. If your program is a subroutine library, you may consider it more useful to permit linking proprietary applications with the library. If this is what you want to do, use the GNU Lesser General Public License instead of this License. But first, please read http://www.gnu.org/philosophy/why-not-lgpl.html.

Contributors to GnuPG

The GnuPG project would like to thank its many contributors. Without them the project would not have been nearly as successful as it has been. Any omissions in this list are accidental. Feel free to contact the maintainer if you have been left out or some of your contributions are not listed.

David Shaw, Matthew Skala, Michael Roth, Niklas Hernaeus, Nils Ellmenreich, Rmi Guyomarch, Stefan Bellon, Timo Schulz and Werner Koch wrote the code. Birger Langkjer, Daniel Resare, Dokianakis Theofanis, Edmund GRIMLEY EVANS, Gal Quri, Gregory Steuck, Nagy Ferenc Lszl, Ivo Timmermans, Jacobo Tarri'o Barreiro, Janusz Aleksander Urbanowicz, Jedi Lin, Jouni Hiltunen, Laurentiu Buzdugan, Magda Procha'zkova', Michael Anckaert, Michal Majer, Marco d'Itri, Nilgun Belma Buguner, Pedro Morais, Tedi Heriyanto, Thiago Jung Bauermann, Rafael Caetano dos Santos, Toomas Soome, Urko Lusa, Walter Koch, Yosiaki IIDA did the official translations. Mike Ashley wrote and maintains the GNU Privacy Handbook. David Scribner is the current FAQ editor. Lorenzo Cappelletti maintains the web site.

The new modularized architecture of gnupg 1.9 as well as the X.509/CMS part has been developed as part of the gypten project. Direct contributors to this project are: Bernhard Herzog, who did extensive testing and tracked down a lot of bugs. Bernhard Reiter, who made sure that we met the specifications and the deadlines. He did extensive testing and came up with a lot of suggestions. Jan-Oliver Wagner made sure that we met the specifications and the deadlines. He also did extensive testing and came up with a lot of suggestions. Karl-Heinz Zimmer and Marc Mutz had to struggle with all the bugs and misconceptions while working on KDE integration. Marcus Brinkman extended GPGME, cleaned up the Assuan code and fixed bugs all over the place. Moritz Schulte took over Libgcrypt maintenance and developed it into a stable an useful library. Steffen Hansen had a hard time to write the dirmngr due to underspecified interfaces. Thomas Koester did extensive testing and tracked down a lot of bugs. Werner Koch designed the system and wrote most of the code.

The following people helped greatly by suggesting improvements, testing, fixing bugs, providing resources and doing other important tasks: Adam Mitchell, Albert Chin, Alec Habig, Allan Clark, Anand Kumria, Andreas Haumer, Anthony Mulcahy, Ariel T Glenn, Bob Mathews, Bodo Moeller, Brendan O'Dea, Brenno de Winter, Brian M. Carlson, Brian Moore, Brian Warner, Bryan Fullerton, Caskey L. Dickson, Cees van de Griend, Charles Levert, Chip Salzenberg, Chris Adams, Christian Biere, Christian Kurz, Christian von Roques, Christopher Oliver, Christian Recktenwald, Dan Winship, Daniel Eisenbud, Daniel Koening, Dave Dykstra, David C Niemi, David Champion, David Ellement, David Hallinan, David Hollenberg, David Mathog, David R. Bergstein, Detlef Lannert, Dimitri, Dirk Lattermann, Dirk Meyer, Disastry, Douglas Calvert, Ed Boraas, Edmund GRIMLEY EVANS, Edwin Woudt, Enzo Michelangeli, Ernst Molitor, Fabio Coatti, Felix von Leitner, fish stiqz, Florian Weimer, Francesco Potorti, Frank Donahoe, Frank Heckenbach, Frank Stajano, Frank Tobin, Gabriel Rosenkoetter, Gal Quri, Gene Carter, Geoff Keating, Georg Schwarz, Giampaolo Tomassoni, Gilbert Fernandes, Greg Louis, Greg Troxel, Gregory Steuck, Gregery Barton, Harald Denker, Holger Baust, Hendrik Buschkamp, Holger Schurig, Holger Smolinski, Holger Trapp, Hugh Daniel, Huy Le, Ian McKellar, Ivo Timmermans, Jan Krueger, Jan Niehusmann, Janusz A. Urbanowicz, James Troup, Jean-loup Gailly, Jeff

Long, Jeffery Von Ronne, Jens Bachem, Jeroen C. van Gelderen, J Horacio MG, J. Michael Ashley, Jim Bauer, Jim Small, Joachim Backes, Joe Rhett, John A. Martin, Johnny Teveen, Jrg Schilling, Jos Backus, Joseph Walton, Juan F. Codagnone, Jun Kuriyama, Kahil D. Jallad, Karl Fogel, Karsten Thygesen, Katsuhiro Kondou, Kazu Yamamoto, Keith Clayton, Kevin Ryde, Klaus Singvogel, Kurt Garloff, Lars Kellogg-Stedman, L. Sassaman, M Taylor, Marcel Waldvogel, Marco d'Itri, Marco Parrone, Marcus Brinkmann, Mark Adler, Mark Elbrecht, Mark Pettit, Markus Friedl, Martin Kahlert, Martin Hamilton, Martin Schulte, Matt Kraai, Matthew Skala, Matthew Wilcox, Matthias Urlichs, Max Valianskiy, Michael Engels, Michael Fischer v. Mollard, Michael Roth, Michael Sobolev, Michael Tokarev, Nicolas Graner, Mike McEwan, Neal H Walfield, Nelson H. F. Beebe, NIIBE Yutaka, Niklas Hernaeus, Nimrod Zimerman, N J Doye, Oliver Haakert, Oskari Jskelinen, Pascal Scheffers, Paul D. Smith, Per Cederqvist, Phil Blundell, Philippe Laliberte, Peter Fales, Peter Gutmann, Peter Marschall, Peter Valchev, Piotr Krukowiecki, QingLong, Ralph Gillen, Rat, Reinhard Wobst, Rmi Guyomarch, Reuben Sumner, Richard Outerbridge, Robert Joop, Roddy Strachan, Roger Sondermann, Roland Rosenfeld, Roman Pavlik, Ross Golder, Ryan Malayter, Sam Roberts, Sami Tolvanen, Sean MacLennan, Sebastian Klemke, Serge Munhoven, SL Baur, Stefan Bellon, Dr.Stefan.Dalibor, Stefan Karrmann, Stefan Keller, Steffen Ullrich, Steffen Zahn, Steven Bakker, Steven Murdoch, Susanne Schultz, Ted Cabeen, Thiago Jung Bauermann, Thijmen Klok, Thomas Roessler, Tim Mooney, Timo Schulz, Todd Vierling, TOGAWA Satoshi, Tom Spindler, Tom Zerucha, Tomas Fasth, Tommi Komulainen, Thomas Klausner, Tomasz Kozlowski, Thomas Mikkelsen, Ulf Mller, Urko Lusa, Vincent P. Broman, Volker Quetschke, W Lewis, Walter Hofmann, Walter Koch, Wayne Chapeskie, Wim Vandeputte, Winona Brown, Yosiaki IIDA, Yoshihiro Kajiki and Gerlinde Klaes.

This software has been made possible by the previous work of Chris Wedgwood, Jeanloup Gailly, Jon Callas, Mark Adler, Martin Hellmann Paul Kendall, Philip R. Zimmermann, Peter Gutmann, Philip A. Nelson, Taher Elgamal, Torbjorn Granlund, Whitfield Diffie, some unknown NSA mathematicians and all the folks who have worked hard to create complete and free operating systems.

And finally we'd like to thank everyone who uses these tools, submits bug reports and generally reminds us why we're doing this work in the first place.

Glossary

'ARL' The *Authority Revocation List* is technical identical to a CRL but used for CAs and not for end user certificates.

'Chain model'
  Verification model for X.509 which uses the creation date of a signature as the date the validation starts and in turn checks that each certificate has been issued within the time frame, the issuing certificate was valid. This allows the verification of signatures after the CA's certificate expired. The validation test also required an online check of the certificate status. The chain model is required by the German signature law. See also *Shell model*.

'CMS' The *Cryptographic Message Standard* describes a message format for encryption and digital signing. It is closely related to the X.509 certificate format. CMS was formerly known under the name PKCS#7 and is described by RFC3369.

'CRL' The *Certificate Revocation List* is a list containing certificates revoked by the issuer.

'CSR' The *Certificate Signing Request* is a message send to a CA to ask them to issue a new certificate. The data format of such a signing request is called PCKS#10.

'OpenPGP' A data format used to build a PKI and to exchange encrypted or signed messages. In contrast to X.509, OpenPGP also includes the message format but does not explicitly demand a specific PKI. However any kind of PKI may be build upon the OpenPGP protocol.

'Keygrip' This term is used by GnuPG to describe a 20 byte hash value used to identify a certain key without referencing to a concrete protocol. It is used internally to access a private key. Usually it is shown and entered as a 40 character hexadecimal formatted string.

'OCSP' The *Online Certificate Status Protocol* is used as an alternative to a CRL. It is described in RFC 2560.

'PSE' The *Personal Security Environment* describes a database to store private keys. This is either a smartcard or a collection of files on a disk; the latter is often called a Soft-PSE.

'Shell model'
  The standard model for validation of certificates under X.509. At the time of the verification all certificates must be valid and not expired. See also *Chain mode*.

'X.509' Description of a PKI used with CMS. It is for example defined by RFC3280.

Option Index

Index